It's more than just about the money—it's about setting yourself up to live a life that's joyful, balanced, and aligned with your values

The 7 Benefits of Retirement Planning

A Practical Guide for People Across All Income Brackets, Whether You're Early in Your Career or Closer to Retirement

Jay Nesbit

MBA / Pharmacist / Award-Winning Author

ALSO BY JAY NESBIT

Rise Above the Rut:

Rediscovering Joy and Purpose in Your Life

Small Changes BIG RESULTS:

Your Guide to Personal Growth and Lasting Happiness

Published by ONE BOOKS LLC - First Edition

ONE BOOKS PUBLISHING
One University Circle – Suite 1402
Cleveland, OH 44106
onebookspublishing@gmail.com

The Seven Benefits of Retirement Planning: A Practical Guide for People Across All Income Brackets, Whether You're Early in Your Career or Closer to Retirement

Library of Congress Control Number: Pending
First Edition – 2025

Professionally Edited by: Diana Bright
Cover and Interior Design by: librovalorempublishing.com

For everyone ready to embrace their journey—this is your moment to shape a retirement filled with meaning, joy, and the freedom to live life on your terms. Let this be the start of something truly extraordinary.

True wealth is not measured by money or possessions, but by the quality of your relationships, health, and sense of purpose

—Unknown

THE SEVEN BENEFITS OF RETIREMENT PLANNING:

Retirement planning isn't just about your future—it can make life better right now too. By having a plan, you'll feel more in control and ready to enjoy both today and tomorrow. The benefits go far beyond just saving money. Here are seven ways planning can boost your life today and set you up for an even better retirement.

1. Reduced Stress and Anxiety

Knowing you have a plan in place can ease the mental load of worrying about the future. You'll feel more in control of your life and finances.

2. More Freedom to Pursue Dreams

With a plan, you'll know when and how you can start exploring things you've always wanted—whether that's travel, hobbies, volunteering, or learning new skills.

3. Stronger Relationships

Planning for retirement gives you the time and space to build stronger bonds with family and friends. Whether it's spending more time with grandkids or reconnecting with old friends, you'll have the opportunity to nurture those relationships.

4. Improved Physical and Mental Health

Without work-related stress, you can focus on self-care. A good retirement plan might include staying active, eating well, and keeping your mind engaged.

5. Purpose and Fulfillment

Retirement doesn't have to mean slowing down. Many people discover new passions, find meaningful volunteer work, or even start a new business. Having a plan helps you stay focused on living with purpose.

6. More Time for Personal Growth

Retirement planning can lead to opportunities for self-discovery and meaningful growth. You'll have time to reflect on your goals, embrace new perspectives, and pursue creative projects.

7. Adaptability for Life Changes

Life is unpredictable, but a strong plan can give you flexibility. You'll be better prepared to handle changes like healthcare needs, relocation, or family responsibilities without feeling overwhelmed.

Planning for retirement means creating a life where you can thrive both now and later. With less stress and more options, you'll be ready to make the most of each chapter of your life. Let's get started!

JAY NESBIT | published by One Books LLC

The 7 Benefits of Retirement Planning

A Practical Guide for People Across All Income Brackets, Whether You're Early in Your Career or Closer to Retirement

A book in the *Life Well Lived* series

Jay Nesbit

TABLE OF CONTENTS

INTRODUCTION

WHY IT'S NEVER TOO EARLY (OR LATE) TO START

A Path to Securing Your Future Without Missing Out on Today

Life moves fast, doesn't it? One moment, you're juggling work deadlines and family dinners; the next, you're wondering where the time went. It's easy to push retirement planning aside with everything else on your plate. But the truth is, the choices you make today—whether you're 25, 50, or 75—can shape your future in big ways.

That's why having a plan is so important. Without one, you might find yourself constantly reacting to life's demands instead of steering toward what truly matters. A plan gives you clarity and control, helping you focus on your goals and adapt when life throws you a curveball.

This book is about more than just financial strategies. It's about creating a life that feels full—financially, physically, and emotionally. You'll get practical tips and read stories of people who found ways to plan confidently, making their lives better today while preparing for tomorrow.

You might be thinking, *"Is it too late to start planning?"* Absolutely not! Whether you're beginning to think about retirement, managing a mid-career balancing act, or already stepping into your retirement years, it's never too late—or too early—to take meaningful steps toward a secure and joyful life.

Together, we'll explore strategies that help you align your retirement plan with your values and dreams. And along the way, you'll read examples of how others balanced life's responsibilities and joys to create the future they wanted.

LIFE IN ACTION

Consider Sarah. In her thirties, she's juggling a demanding career, raising two kids, and diligently saving for the future. But Sarah knows life isn't just about responsibilities. She's also making time for the things that bring her joy—gardening and taking family trips that create lasting memories. This book helped her strike that tricky balance between planning for tomorrow and living fully today.

Then there's Mark, in his fifties. Building his business has always been his top priority, and retirement planning felt like something he'd tackle "later." With the help of this guide, Mark realized retirement isn't just about piling up money—it's about creating a clear picture of the life he wants after stepping away from work and taking intentional steps now to make that dream a reality.

And let's not forget Helen, in her seventies. For her, this book became more than just a financial tool. It inspired her to fine-tune her finances and rediscover her passions—painting and volunteering. Helen's journey reminds us that no matter what your age, it's never too late to shape a retirement that secures your future while reigniting your sense of purpose and joy.

These stories show that retirement planning isn't just about numbers—it's about designing a life that reflects what truly matters to you, at every stage.

More Than Just Financials

Sure, we'll dig into the financial side—after all, having a solid plan is key. But retirement planning is about much more than just money. It's about living a life that's full and meaningful. It's about your well-being, your relationships, and the things that truly bring you joy.

Retirement isn't simply about walking away from work. It's an opportunity to step into a new chapter full of possibilities. Whether that means taking on part-time work, diving into a passion project, or slowing down to enjoy life's little moments, this is your chance to design a future that feels right for *you.*

This book will guide you toward striking that balance between financial security and the freedom to pursue what makes you happiest. It's not just about getting to the next phase—it's about loving that phase and living fully. Because at the end of the day, retirement planning isn't just about having a plan. It's about creating a life that feels as good as it looks on paper.

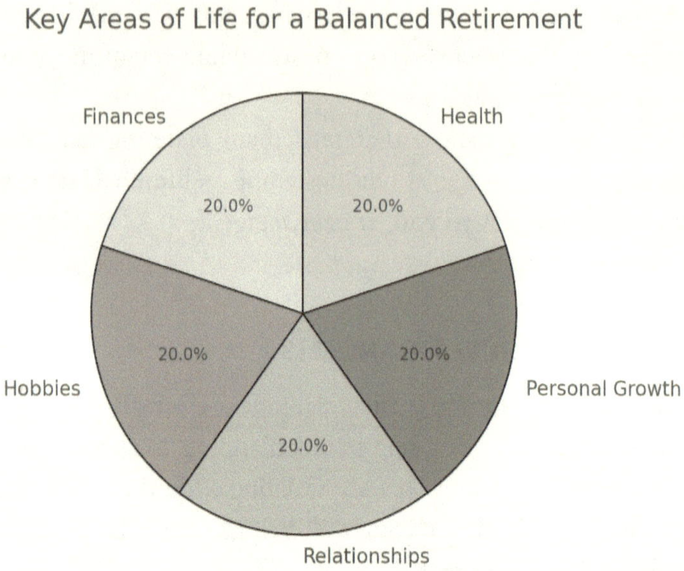

Understanding the Chart Above

This pie chart highlights the key areas that contribute to a balanced retirement: Finances, Health, Personal Growth, Relationships, and Hobbies. Each slice of the pie carries equal weight, emphasizing the importance of enriching every aspect of your life.

By paying attention to all these areas, you can build a retirement that's not just financially secure but also deeply rewarding. It's about creating a life where every part feels rich and meaningful. Think of this chart as a visual reminder that true wealth isn't only about money—it's about thriving in every corner of your life.

PULLING IT ALL TOGETHER

Planning for retirement means more than just checking financial boxes. It's about creating a future where you can thrive—living with joy, purpose, and security. Whether your goal is to travel, spend time with loved ones, or dive into passions you've put on hold, this book will guide you there.

No matter where you are in your journey, you can take meaningful steps today to shape the retirement you deserve. So, let's get started—because your best years are still ahead!

A QUICK TAKEAWAY:

A life well-lived is one where you've balanced work, wealth, joy, and purpose—each step you take brings you closer.

PART 1

CHAPTER ONE

LAYING THE GROUNDWORK IN YOUR TWENTIES

Laying the Groundwork for a Secure Future

Your twenties are an exciting time, filled with new opportunities, career beginnings, and personal growth. Even though retirement may feel like a far-off concern, this is actually the perfect time to start laying a strong foundation for your future.

In this chapter, we'll dive into essential elements such as setting financial goals, developing healthy habits, making thoughtful career choices, building a supportive network, and embracing lifelong learning. These are all key ingredients for creating a fulfilling and secure retirement.

To bring these concepts to life, we'll start with Amina's story—a relatable and inspiring journey through her twenties. Her experiences highlight the common challenges and aspirations many of us encounter while navigating the early stages of adulthood and setting the stage for the years ahead.

Life in Action: Amina in Her Twenties

Meet Amina, a 23-year-old who recently earned her bachelor's degree in business and is about to start her career. As the first in her family to graduate from college, Amina feels a deep sense of pride and responsibility. Her parents have worked hard to support the family—her mother as a nursing assistant and her father as an electrician. They live in a modest home with a mortgage and couldn't contribute significantly to her college tuition.

Amina's determination and grit carried her through school, but she graduated with nearly $50,000 in student debt, despite receiving scholarships and grants. She also has $15,000 in credit card debt and just $200 in savings.

With a major in economics, Amina has landed a promising position as a Junior Business Data Analyst at a Fortune 500 company, earning a starting salary of $75,000 per year. She's set clear financial goals: sharing an apartment with friends who are also starting their careers, saving or borrowing to buy a reliable used car, setting aside funds for graduate courses, and tackling her debts. She also wants to learn more about budgeting, saving, and investing to better manage her finances.

Your twenties are a vibrant, transitional time, much like Amina's. It's a period filled with excitement, new beginnings, and challenges as you navigate life after school or discover what excites you most. Retirement may seem like a distant concern at this stage, and it's natural to wonder why you should think about it now when you're just finding your footing in adulthood.

But here's the key: your twenties are the perfect time to plant the seeds for your financial future, just like planting a tree. The earlier you start, the more it can grow and provide the shade you'll need later in life. Let's explore the essential steps you can take now to build a strong foundation for retirement planning and beyond.

Setting Financial Goals for a Secure Future

You've likely heard the saying, "If you fail to plan, you plan to fail." This is especially true when it comes to retirement. Setting financial goals is the essential first step on your path to a secure future. Like Amina, you need a clear plan with specific objectives. These goals will act as guideposts, shaping your financial decisions, influencing key choices, and ultimately impacting your quality of life over the years.

Here's how to approach financial goal-setting in your twenties:

Define Your Retirement Age

When do you see yourself retiring? Your desired retirement age will greatly influence how much you need to save and the strategies you use to invest. The average retirement age in the U.S. is currently 61, but if early retirement appeals to you, you'll need to save more aggressively and make smart investment decisions. On the other hand, retiring later allows for additional contributions over a longer period, potentially easing your savings burden.

Calculate Your Retirement Income Needs

How much will you need annually in retirement to maintain your desired lifestyle? Factor in expenses such as housing, transportation, healthcare, leisure activities, and other priorities. For reference, *The Motley Fool* suggests aiming for an annual retirement income of $96,000 (in 2024 dollars) for a comfortable lifestyle.

Compare that to the 2024 average monthly Social Security benefit of $1,862 (about $22,000 annually)—a figure that leaves little room for anything beyond basic expenses. This underscores the importance of diversifying your income sources, such as through investments, to secure financial stability.

Remember to adjust your retirement income targets yearly to account for inflation, ensuring your plan stays realistic and relevant.

Assess Your Current Financial Situation

Start with an honest evaluation of where you stand. What are your assets, debts, and income?

- **Assets** are what you own, like savings, investments, and property.
- **Debts** (or liabilities) are what you owe, such as student loans or credit card balances.
- **Income** is the money you bring in from your job, side gigs, or other sources.

This step gives you a clear snapshot of your financial health and identifies areas that need improvement. Create a personal balance sheet listing your assets and liabilities. Think of it as a financial report card where you're in charge of improving the grade.

Estimate Your Life Expectancy

While no one can predict their exact lifespan, planning for a longer retirement is wise. The current average life expectancy in the U.S. is 77, but aiming for a projection closer to 90 offers a more cautious approach.

It's like packing for a long trip—you'd rather overpack than run out of essentials halfway through. Preparing for a longer life ensures your savings last, even if you outlive the averages.

Set Short-Term and Long-Term Goals

Breaking your goals into short-term and long-term categories helps make them more manageable and focused. But what's the difference?

Short-term goals are objectives you can achieve within a few months to a couple of years. These focus on building a foundation for your financial health and tackling immediate priorities. Examples include:

- **Building an emergency fund** ensures you have cash readily available for unexpected expenses, giving you peace of mind in the short run.
- **Paying off high-interest debt** reduces financial strain and frees up money for other goals.
- **Starting monthly retirement contributions** gets you in the habit of saving early, which is essential for long-term success but starts with manageable, immediate steps.

Long-term goals take several years or even decades to accomplish. They're about creating security and achieving major milestones. Examples include:

- **Saving for a home** requires careful planning and significant savings over time.
- **Hitting a retirement savings target** spans decades and requires consistent effort.
- **Diversifying your investments** builds wealth over the long haul, helping you weather market changes and grow your portfolio sustainably.

Short-term goals provide the immediate stability needed to build a strong financial foundation, while long-term goals give you a clear vision of the future and ensure you're prepared for major life events, like retirement or buying a home. Both are critical, and understanding their differences ensures you're balancing today's needs with tomorrow's dreams.

Manage Student Debt

If you have student loans, develop a clear repayment plan to free up more money for retirement savings. Think of it as clearing financial clutter. Options like income-driven repayment plans or refinancing to lower interest rates can ease the burden. Automating payments simplifies the process and ensures consistent progress.

Adjust Your Goals as You Progress

Life is full of surprises, and your financial goals should adapt accordingly. Whether it's a career change, a significant income increase, or unexpected life events, revisiting and revising your plan ensures you stay aligned with your evolving priorities. Regular check-ins keep you on track toward your ultimate goals.

In Summary

Your twenties are the perfect time to begin saving for retirement. The magic of compound interest means even small contributions now can grow significantly over time. By setting ambitious yet achievable goals, you're creating a solid foundation for a secure and fulfilling future. Every step you take today is an investment in the life you want tomorrow.

Retirement Planning Sheet

Step 1: Define Your Retirement Age

1. Desired Retirement Age
2. Current Age
3. Years Until Retirement - Subtract current age from desired retirement age

Step 2: Calculate Your Retirement Income Needs

1. Desired Annual Income in Retirement
2. Estimated Years in Retirement - Use your life expectancy minus your desired retirement age
3. Total Retirement Income Needed: - Multiply desired annual income by estimated years in retirement

Step 3: Assess Your Current Financial Situation

1. Current Savings
2. Current Debt
3. Net Worth - Savings minus Debt

Step 4: Estimate Your Life Expectancy

1. Estimated Life Expectancy in Years
2. Estimated Years in Retirement - Subtract desired retirement age from estimated life expectancy

Step 5: Set Short-Term and Long-Term Goals

Short-Term Goals:

1. Build an Emergency Fund
2. Pay Off High-Interest Debt
3. Contribute Monthly to Retirement Account

Long-Term Goals:

1. Save for a Down Payment on a House
2. Establish Retirement Savings Target
3. Develop a Diversified Investment Portfolio

Step 6: Manage Student Debt

1. Total Student Debt
2. Monthly Payment Plan -If applicable
3. Debt-Free Target Date

Step 7: Adjust Your Goals as You Progress

1. Annual Review Date
2. Notes for Adjustments

Understanding the Planning Sheet Above

This Retirement Planning Sheet breaks the process into easy-to-follow steps, helping you take a closer look at your financial future. Each section is designed to guide you through defining your retirement age, calculating income needs, assessing your current financial situation, and setting short- and long-term goals.

By completing this sheet, you'll have a clearer picture of where you stand financially and what actions are needed to achieve your retirement dreams. It's not just about the numbers; it's about aligning your finances with your personal vision for retirement.

This tool is invaluable because it turns abstract ideas into actionable steps. It ensures you're actively planning for a secure and fulfilling retirement, rather than leaving it to chance. Starting today means more control over your financial future and greater confidence in reaching your goals.

Health and Wellness: Establishing Healthy Habits Early

Good health is one of the most valuable assets you can have—just ask someone who lacks it. Your twenties are a critical time to establish healthy habits that will benefit you throughout your life and enhance your quality of life in retirement. It's not just about looking and feeling good; it's also about reducing healthcare costs and supporting long-term well-being.

Here's how to start building a foundation of healthy habits early:

Stay Physically Active

Regular exercise can boost your overall well-being, reduce the risk of chronic diseases, and improve mental health. Find activities you enjoy and make them a consistent part of your routine.

- Consider a daily 30-minute walk in nature or activities like jogging, yoga, or team sports.
- The key is choosing something you look forward to and can maintain over time.

Maintain a Balanced Diet

Eating well in your twenties lays the groundwork for a healthy metabolism and lasting nutritional habits.

- Focus on a diet rich in fruits, vegetables, lean proteins, and whole grains.
- Consult a dietitian to create a meal plan tailored to your needs and preferences.
- Limit snacks and sugary drinks—they may be tempting, but moderation is key to feeling your best.

Stay Hydrated and Get Enough Sleep

Hydration and sleep are essential for both physical and mental health.

- Aim for 7–9 hours of sleep each night and drink plenty of water throughout the day.
- Maintaining a consistent sleep schedule and staying hydrated will leave you feeling more energetic and focused.

Avoid Harmful Habits

Now is the time to break harmful habits like smoking or excessive alcohol consumption.

- These behaviors not only jeopardize your health but also drain your finances.
- For strategies to overcome unhealthy patterns, refer to my first book, *Rise Above the Rut.* Seek support from friends, family, or professional resources as needed.

Prioritize Regular Check-Ups and Preventative Care

Regular medical check-ups help catch potential health issues early and reduce medical costs over time.

- Schedule annual physicals, dental check-ups, and eye exams.
- Think of preventative care as maintenance for your body—routine visits can help you avoid major health problems down the line.

Support Mental and Emotional Wellness

Managing stress, practicing mindfulness, and nurturing relationships are just as important as physical health.

- Try practices like meditation, journaling, or therapy to maintain mental health.
- Building resilience and a positive outlook can enhance your quality of life and make navigating future challenges easier.

Manage Your Finances and Lifestyle

Financial stability has a direct impact on stress levels and overall health.

- Create a budget, track spending, and avoid unnecessary debt to improve your financial well-being.
- Use budgeting tools or apps to stay organized and on track with your goals.

By focusing on these areas, you'll create a solid foundation of healthy habits that will serve you well throughout your life. Taking care of your health now increases the likelihood of enjoying a more vibrant, fulfilling retirement in the future.

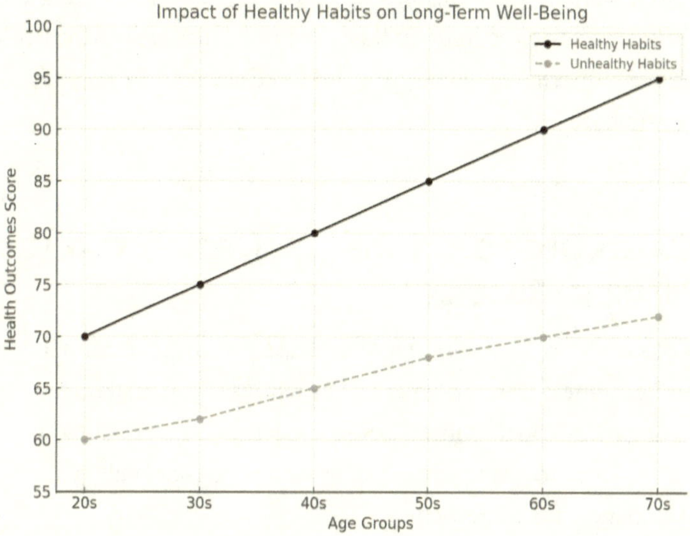

Understanding the Chart Above

This chart highlights the long-term benefits of maintaining healthy habits across different age groups. The **solid line** represents individuals who consistently engage in regular exercise, follow a balanced diet, and get adequate sleep, showcasing significantly higher health outcomes as they age.

In contrast, the **dashed line** reflects those who neglect these habits, resulting in lower health outcomes over time. Starting healthy habits in your twenties greatly improves your well-being, reduces the risk of chronic diseases, and lowers healthcare costs. These proactive steps contribute to a more fulfilling and financially secure retirement.

In Summary

Establishing healthy habits isn't about striving for perfection—it's about making steady progress. Think of it as a gift to your future self. By prioritizing your health now, you're setting the foundation for a retirement that's not only financially secure but also rich in vitality, giving you the freedom to fully enjoy life's possibilities.

Career Decisions: Laying the Groundwork for Financial Success

Your career plays a critical role in shaping your financial stability and readiness for retirement. The choices you make early in your professional journey can significantly impact your future. Here's how to make smart career decisions that build a strong foundation for retirement:

Choose a Career with Growth Potential

Look for opportunities in industries with strong demand and roles that offer advancement and salary growth. Research career paths that align with your interests but also provide financial stability. Pursue certifications or advanced degrees to enhance your earning potential and open doors for career advancement.

Negotiate Your Salary

Never shy away from negotiating your salary, whether at the start of a new job or during performance reviews. Research industry standards and be prepared to showcase your accomplishments and value. The U.S. Bureau of Labor Statistics can provide helpful salary data, giving you factual backup for your discussions. Think of salary negotiation as getting extra toppings on your pizza—why settle for less when you can have more?

Invest in Continuous Education

Lifelong learning boosts your skills and keeps you competitive. Take advantage of workshops, training programs, or online courses to stay current in your field. Staying updated on industry trends and new technology gives you an edge and can open new opportunities, ensuring your career remains dynamic and adaptable.

Build a Professional Network

Networking is a powerful tool for career growth. Attend industry events, join online communities, and connect with professionals in your field. Networking can lead to mentorship, advice from seasoned professionals, and even job opportunities you wouldn't otherwise hear about.

Consider Work-Life Balance

While advancing your career is important, maintaining a healthy work-life balance is equally crucial. A job that monopolizes your time and energy can take a toll on your health and personal life. Seek roles that allow you to pursue your professional goals while leaving room for personal interests and well-being.

Save and Invest Wisely

Start saving and investing early to take advantage of compound interest. Participate in employer-sponsored retirement plans, like a 401(k), and consider opening an

Individual Retirement Account (IRA). Consulting a financial advisor is like using GPS for your finances—helping you avoid wrong turns and stay on track for your goals. A solid strategy now means fewer financial worries in the future.

Plan for Career Transitions

Be ready for potential career changes or transitions, whether it's shifting to a new industry, pursuing a different role, or starting your own business. Develop transferable skills that can be applied to various roles or industries to keep your options open. Preparing for unexpected shifts increases your ability to navigate challenges smoothly while maintaining financial stability.

Smart career decisions now will not only boost your earning potential but also position you for long-term financial success. By focusing on growth, balance, and adaptability, you'll create a career that supports your goals both today and into retirement.

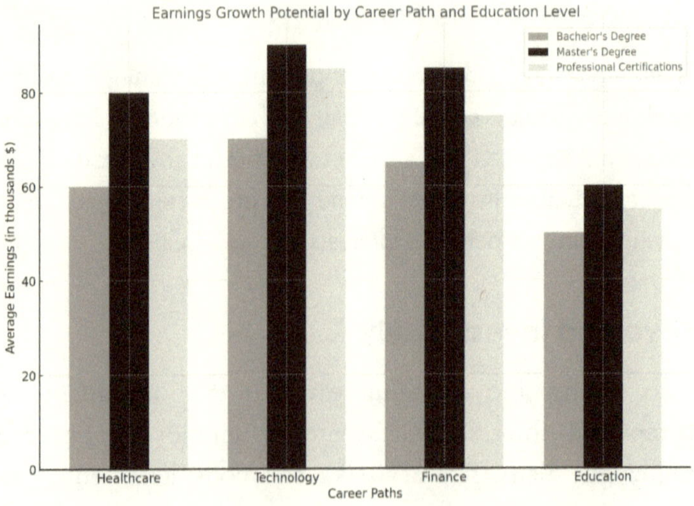

Understanding the Chart Above

This bar chart compares potential earnings growth across various career paths—healthcare, technology, finance, and education—based on levels of education: bachelor's degree, master's degree, and professional certifications. The data highlights how investing in further education and skill development can lead to significantly higher earnings over time.

Higher income not only improves your current financial stability but also boosts your ability to save and invest for retirement. This creates a stronger financial foundation for your future, ensuring you're better equipped to meet long-term goals and enjoy a secure retirement.

In Summary

Your career decisions directly impact your financial trajectory. By choosing paths that offer growth, prioritizing continuous education, and strategically managing your career, you can position yourself to achieve your financial goals. The payoff? A retirement with more beach days and fewer "work-from-home" days!

Building a Supportive Network: The Importance of Relationships

In addition to financial planning, it's important to build a supportive network to help you grow personally and professionally. Surrounding yourself with people who have a positive impact on your life can offer guidance, encouragement, and opportunities to boost your success and well-being.

Here's how to build and maintain a strong network:

Surround Yourself with Positive People

Build relationships with people who inspire and encourage you. These supportive connections can offer helpful advice, motivation, and a boost of confidence as you work toward your goals. Spend time with individuals who share your values and dreams and who can help you grow both personally and professionally.

Cultivate Meaningful Relationships

Focus on building meaningful connections rather than simply expanding your network. Quality relationships with mentors, friends, and colleagues offer deeper support and guidance. It's not about adding names to your contact list—it's about forming genuine connections that matter. Take time to nurture these relationships and remember to offer support in return. True friends are worth more than a stack of business cards.

Seek Out Mentorship

A mentor can provide valuable insights and advice based on their experiences. Look for mentors who have achieved success in your field or can guide you on your career and financial goals. Build a relationship with someone who can offer constructive feedback and support your growth.

Participate in Professional Organizations

Joining professional organizations in your field provides networking opportunities, access to industry resources, and avenues for professional development. Attend events, conferences, and workshops to connect with others in your industry and stay informed about trends and advancements.

Give Back to Your Community

Contributing to your community through volunteering or mentoring creates meaningful connections and builds goodwill. Giving back also brings a sense of fulfillment and purpose, enhancing your overall well-being.

Communicate Openly and Honestly

Effective communication is key to building strong relationships. Be open and honest with your network, and be willing to listen and support others. Building trust and mutual respect strengthens connections and leads to more meaningful interactions.

Leverage Social Media and Online Platforms

Social media and online platforms are valuable tools for expanding your network and staying connected. Think of platforms like LinkedIn as your digital handshake. Use them to connect with professionals in your field, share achievements, and engage with industry-related content. Remember, it's about building genuine connections—not just collecting likes.

In Summary

By surrounding yourself with positive influences and nurturing meaningful relationships, you create a strong foundation for achieving your goals and enjoying a fulfilling retirement. A supportive network enriches your personal and professional life, offering guidance and encouragement every step of the way.

Embracing Lifelong Learning: Staying Curious and Informed

Lifelong learning is essential for both personal and professional growth. Continuously seeking knowledge and new experiences sharpens your skills, keeps you adaptable, and contributes to long-term success. Here are practical ways to embrace lifelong learning in your twenties:

Pursue Further Education

Consider advancing your career through additional degrees or certifications. Continuing education equips you with specialized knowledge and skills that distinguish you in your field. Options like online courses, workshops, and professional development programs make learning accessible and flexible.

Read Regularly

Make reading a habit to expand your knowledge and stay updated on current trends. Explore books, articles, and journals related to your field and personal interests. Broaden your perspective by diving into a variety of genres, from self-improvement to fiction. Reading is not just about learning—it's also a source of inspiration and creativity.

Attend Workshops and Seminars

Participate in workshops, seminars, and conferences to gain new skills and insights. These events are valuable for networking, hands-on learning, and hearing from industry experts. Think of them as skill-building boot camps, often with the bonus of coffee breaks and free snacks. Look for events aligned with your career or personal passions.

Learn from Experiences

View every challenge and new experience as an opportunity to grow. Whether it's a work project, a volunteer role, or a personal goal, approach it with curiosity and openness. Reflect on what you've learned and how it contributes to your overall development.

Seek Feedback and Mentorship

Constructive feedback is one of the most powerful tools for growth. Actively seek input from colleagues, mentors, and peers to identify areas for improvement. A good mentor provides guidance and real-world insights, helping you navigate your career and personal aspirations more effectively.

Stay Updated on Industry Trends

Keep up with advancements in your field by subscribing to industry publications, following thought leaders, and engaging in online communities. Staying informed not only enhances your expertise but also ensures you remain competitive in your career.

Develop New Hobbies and Interests

Lifelong learning isn't limited to your profession. Explore hobbies and interests outside of work to boost creativity, reduce stress, and find fulfillment. Whether it's cooking, hiking, or learning a new language, hobbies provide a refreshing break from routine while enriching your life.

In Summary

Embracing lifelong learning is about more than just acquiring knowledge—it's about growing as a person. By staying curious and informed, you'll be better equipped to handle challenges, seize opportunities, and achieve both personal and professional goals. Keep learning, and the world will always have something new to offer!

Closing Thoughts

Your twenties are a critical time to set the stage for your future. By focusing on clear financial goals, healthy habits, smart career choices, meaningful relationships, and continuous learning, you're building the foundation for a balanced and fulfilling retirement.

Whether you choose to pursue a college degree or not, the principles in this guide apply to everyone. Smart financial decisions, career growth, and personal development aren't limited by educational background. You have the power to create a secure and prosperous future by seeking opportunities, making wise financial choices, and maintaining balance as you work toward your dreams.

Like Amina, you can shape your future through thoughtful decisions and proactive steps during this pivotal decade. The actions you take now will have a lasting impact on your financial security, health, and overall well-being. It's never too early to start planning for the life you want in the years ahead.

Take charge of your future with confidence. Remember, the journey to a secure retirement begins with the decisions you make today. Future you will thank present you for taking that first step. Building your future isn't just about numbers—it's about creating a life filled with joy, purpose, and possibility.

So, go ahead—lace up your shoes and stride confidently through your twenties. Every smart decision you make now is a step closer to the life you've always imagined.

Resources for Further Learning

To dive deeper into the topics covered in this chapter and strengthen your understanding of retirement planning, personal finance, career development, and lifelong learning, consider exploring these additional resources:

Books:

1. **"The Millionaire Next Door: The Surprising Secrets of America's Wealthy"** by Thomas J. Stanley and William D. Danko. This classic book explores the habits and traits of America's wealthiest individuals and offers practical advice for building wealth over time.
2. **"Your Money or Your Life: 9 Steps to Transforming Your Relationship with Money and Achieving Financial Independence"** by Vicki Robin and Joe Dominguez - A comprehensive guide to managing finances, this

book helps you align your spending with your values and achieve financial independence.

3. **"The Total Money Makeover: A Proven Plan for Financial Fitness"** by Dave Ramsey - Dave Ramsey provides a step-by-step plan for managing debt, saving money, and investing for the future.
4. **"The Bogleheads' Guide to Retirement Planning"** by Mel Lindauer, Taylor Larimore, and Michael LeBoeuf - This guide offers practical advice on retirement planning, including investment strategies and saving tips.

Workshops and Seminars:

1. **Local Financial Planning Workshops -** Many community centers, libraries, and financial institutions offer workshops on retirement planning, budgeting, and investing. Check with local organizations for upcoming events.
2. **Online Webinars -** Websites like Coursera, Udemy, and Khan Academy offer webinars and courses on personal finance, career development, and lifelong learning.

Professional Organizations:

1. **National Association of Personal Financial Advisors (NAPFA) -** Provides resources and directories to find certified financial planners who can help with retirement planning and financial advice.

2. **American Management Association (AMA) -** Offers professional development resources and workshops for career growth and skill enhancement.

These resources will help you deepen your knowledge and support your journey toward a secure and fulfilling retirement. Explore them to gain insights, strategies, and inspiration as you build your retirement foundation and prepare for the future.

A Quick Takeaway:

The seeds you plant in your twenties will grow into the trees that shade your retirement.

YOUR SPECIAL GIFT OFFER: WIN A FREE AUTOGRAPHED BOOK!

Thank you for purchasing *The 7 Benefits of Retirement Planning*! As a token of my appreciation, I'm thrilled to offer you an exclusive chance to win a **signed copy** of one of my two award-winning books: *Rise Above the Rut* or *Small Changes Big Results*.

Here's how it works:

- **24 autographed copies are available**.
- Winners are chosen **randomly every month** while supplies last.
- It's completely **FREE to enter**—just register below!
- **PLUS, THERE'S MORE:**

Also, when you sign up, you'll also receive my **"Life-Changing Words"** blog posts straight to your inbox, twice a month. Each post is packed with practical tips, inspiring stories, and actionable advice to help you live a life of purpose and joy.

Take the next step:

Don't miss out on this exciting opportunity! Whether you're looking to create a purposeful life or add an inspiring read to your bookshelf, make sure to register now for your chance to win a free autographed book.

Scan the QR code below to register for your chance to win a free autographed book and receive twice-monthly blog posts filled with inspiration and practical tips. Don't miss this incredible opportunity!

Or visit my website at: https://www.jaynesbit.com/contact

YOUR FREE GIFT

As a way of saying thanks for your purchase, I'm offering the ***Welcome to Your Planning, Living, and Thriving in Retirement Cheat Sheet*** for **FREE** to my readers.

Get instant access!

https://tinyurl.com/FreeResourceDownload

Inside the Free Cheat Sheet, you will discover:

- **Retirement Clarity** – Define your vision and create a plan that fits your goals.
- **Financial Confidence** – Budget, save, and invest wisely for a secure future.
- **Meaningful Living** – Stay active, engaged, and fulfilled in retirement.

If you want practical strategies to plan, live, and thrive in retirement with less stress and more purpose, make sure to grab the free book.

CHAPTER TWO

CHARTING YOUR COURSE IN YOUR THIRTIES

Expanding Your Vision in Your Thirties

With your twenties in the rearview mirror, it's time to step confidently into your thirties—a defining decade that can shape the rest of your life. In this chapter, we'll build on the foundation you've already laid, offering practical tips to further prepare for retirement while enjoying the journey.

Your thirties are about more than just financial planning. This is a decade of balancing career growth, family responsibilities, maintaining your health, and strengthening support systems. It's also a time to master the art of living in the moment while securing your future.

Let's make sure you're on the right path to building a retirement you'll truly enjoy, while also making the most of the present. After all, the best plans strike a balance between preparing for the future and embracing the moments that bring joy and meaning to your life right now.

Life in Action: David and Jill in Their Thirties

Let's explore the lives of David and Jill, a couple in their early thirties, as they navigate the path toward a fulfilling retirement. Married for three years, they face both opportunities and challenges at this exciting stage of life.

David, a dedicated pharmacist with five years of experience at a local hospital, is focused on advancing his career. He recently enrolled in an MBA program to unlock management roles that will bring him personal fulfillment and strengthen their financial future. His commitment to career growth and education is laying the groundwork for long-term financial security.

Jill, a skilled surgical technician, stepped into the role of stay-at-home mom following the birth of their second child earlier this year. She treasures her time with their newborn and plans to return to work in a few years. Jill values her professional skills and understands how her career can contribute to the family's income and overall retirement planning.

In addition to managing their careers and family responsibilities, David and Jill have been diligently handling their finances. They saved purposefully for a down payment and became proud homeowners last year. However, they are also addressing financial challenges. They currently have $20,000 in credit card debt, mostly from a vacation and furnishing their new home. To tackle this, they've created a detailed plan to manage and eliminate their debt.

For retirement, David contributes 3% of his income to his workplace retirement plan, with plans to gradually increase this percentage over time. The couple currently has two cars with loans and is actively working to pay them off while keeping their broader financial goals on track.

With the addition of their infant son and his two-year-old brother, David and Jill experience immense joy but also face significant financial responsibilities. They are budgeting carefully for childcare, education, and healthcare expenses. Additionally, they've reviewed their health, life, and disability insurance policies to protect their family from unforeseen events.

David and Jill are committed to enhancing their financial literacy, with a focus on saving, budgeting, and investing wisely. They prioritize balancing work and family life, striving to grow their income while ensuring they have quality time for personal pursuits and relaxation. They recognize that achieving this balance is critical not only for their thirties but also for building a secure and fulfilling future.

KEY DECISIONS ON YOUR PATH TOWARD A PROSPEROUS RETIREMENT

Your thirties are a prime time to solidify the foundation for a secure retirement. This section outlines practical strategies to help you advance your career, enhance your skills, master salary negotiations, and explore entrepreneurial opportunities. Each decision you make now plays a crucial role in shaping a comfortable and well-deserved retirement.

Pursue Career Advancement

Your thirties are an excellent time to focus on career growth. Take on additional responsibilities and aim for promotions to increase your income and strengthen your retirement planning foundation.

The skills you develop now can directly impact your family's financial stability and help avoid surprises later. Smart career decisions today set you up for a future where you're working smarter, not harder.

Invest in Skill Development

In today's fast-changing job market, continuous learning is essential. Attend workshops, join professional organizations, or enroll in college courses to grow your skills, expand your knowledge, and stay competitive in your field.

For example, David is enhancing his pharmacy career by pursuing an MBA, while Jill stays updated on surgical technician skills through industry journals as she prepares to return to work. These investments in skill development can open doors to new opportunities and boost your earning potential.

Negotiate Your Salary

Don't hesitate to negotiate your salary as your responsibilities grow—it's not just about earning more today. A higher income now can accelerate your savings, reduce financial stress, and provide a stronger foundation for your retirement future.

Approach salary discussions with a well-prepared summary of your accomplishments and the value you bring to your organization. Use specific examples and market data to justify your request. Negotiation isn't just about the money—it's about recognizing and rewarding your growing expertise.

Seek New Challenges

Embrace new challenges in your current role to build skills and stand out to employers. Volunteer for projects that push you beyond your comfort zone and uncover new opportunities.

Attend workshops or industry events to expand your knowledge and network with peers. These proactive steps not only keep your work life engaging but also prepare you for roles you might not have previously considered.

Consider Entrepreneurship

Starting your own business or side hustle can diversify your income and provide financial stability over time.

For example, you might explore consulting or selling a product related to a passion or expertise. Entrepreneurship allows you to leverage your skills in a way that's both enjoyable and profitable, offering additional financial security and flexibility.

Maintain Work-Life Balance

Striking a balance between work and personal life is essential to prevent burnout and maintain overall well-being.

Prioritize quality time for family, personal interests, and relaxation. Learn to set boundaries at work and say "no" to excessive overtime or shifts when necessary. A healthier balance ensures that your career doesn't overshadow other important aspects of your life.

By focusing on these key areas in your thirties, you'll be better positioned for financial stability, career satisfaction, and personal fulfillment. Each step you take now brings you closer to a prosperous retirement while ensuring you enjoy the journey along the way.

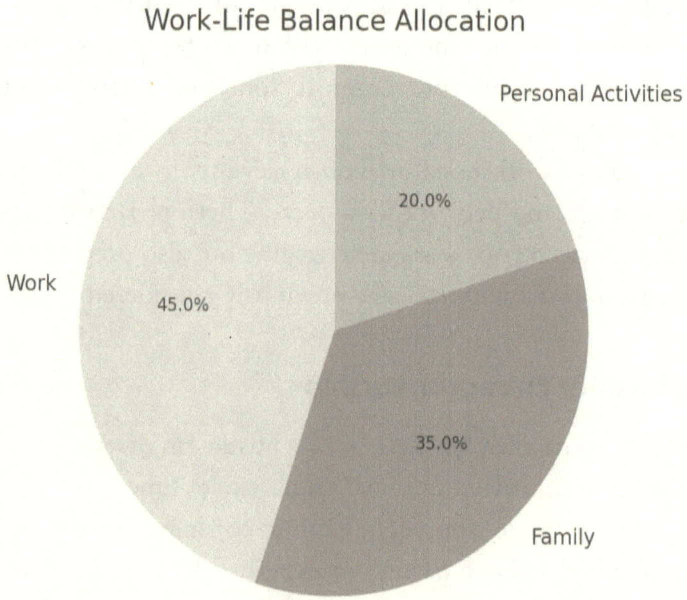

Understanding the Chart Above

This pie chart provides a snapshot of how time is typically allocated between work, family, and personal activities. The largest portion is often dedicated to work, followed by family time, with personal activities making up the smallest slice.

The chart highlights the need for conscious time management to achieve a healthy work-life balance. By identifying how your time is divided, you can make thoughtful adjustments to prioritize personal well-being and nurture family relationships—both essential for long-term happiness and success.

In Summary

We've covered career growth, entrepreneurship, and maintaining balance in your thirties. Next, we'll explore a key aspect of retirement preparation: family planning. Whether you're starting a family or managing current responsibilities, careful financial and lifestyle planning is fundamental to building a prosperous and fulfilling future.

Family Planning and the Financial Implications

Planning for a family in your thirties is like giving your finances a grown-up pep talk. This stage involves practical aspects of family planning, from budgeting for parenting to securing insurance and saving for education. It's not just about managing the present; it's about securing your family's future—a key component of your broader retirement strategy. Let's break down the essentials of family financial planning in straightforward terms.

Prepare Financially for Parenthood

Embracing the joys of parenthood also brings additional financial responsibilities. Start by budgeting carefully for childcare, education, and healthcare expenses to strengthen your financial preparedness.

For instance, consider allocating a specific portion of your budget to these areas. Creating a financial buffer can help protect you from unexpected strains. Setting up a separate savings account specifically for child-related expenses can make managing these costs more effective. Remember, while focusing on your family, it's essential to keep long-term savings goals, such as retirement and future housing needs, in view.

Review and Adjust Insurance Coverage

As your family grows, take the time to review your insurance coverage. Ensure your policies include health, life, disability, homeowners or renters, auto, and an umbrella policy to safeguard against unexpected challenges.

Examine your life insurance policy to confirm it adequately meets your family's needs. Consider adding or increasing disability coverage, especially if your household relies on a single income. Strengthening your insurance strategy now provides added security and peace of mind. If you're uncertain about your coverage, consulting an insurance advisor can help you create a tailored plan.

Create a Family Budget

A family budget is more than just tracking where your money goes—it's a tool to create financial stability and peace of mind for your family. Start by accounting for both immediate expenses and future needs.

Make sure to include essentials like groceries, housing, and transportation, but also set aside money for priorities like emergencies, education, and long-term goals. An emergency fund acts as a safety net for unexpected expenses, while saving for future needs, such as retirement or a home, keeps you on track for bigger milestones.

Regularly review and adjust your budget to reflect life's changes, whether it's a new job, growing kids, or shifting priorities. By taking a proactive approach to your family's finances, you'll not only manage day-to-day expenses but also build a secure foundation for the future—without losing sight of long-term goals like retirement.

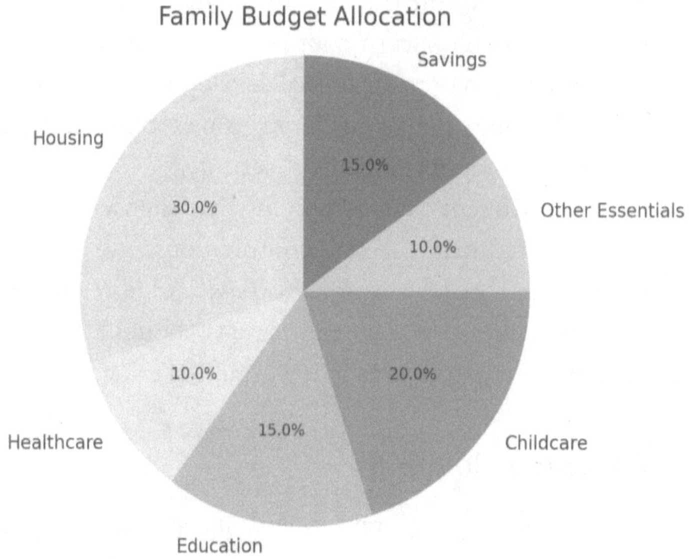

Understanding the Chart Above

This pie chart illustrates a typical family budget allocation in your thirties, with categories such as childcare, education, healthcare, housing, savings, and daily essentials. It highlights how most of your budget is distributed, emphasizing the importance of thoughtful planning.

By visualizing how your finances are divided, you can better manage current expenses while also preparing for the future. The goal is to create a financial safety net that provides peace of mind, enabling you to plan confidently and enjoy life without constant money stress.

Save for Education Costs

If you have children, start saving for their education as early as possible. Options like 529 plans, which are tax-advantaged accounts specifically designed for education expenses, can help your savings grow over time. Even small contributions made consistently can add up significantly.

If children aren't part of your plan, consider saving for your own education or professional development. Investing in lifelong learning can open doors to new opportunities and boost your long-term financial security.

Explore different savings options that align with your goals, and automate your contributions to ensure consistency and make saving effortless. Additionally, as college approaches, students and parents should look into scholarships and grants to help lower tuition costs.

Revisit Estate Planning

As your family grows, revisit and update your estate planning. A will outlines how your assets will be distributed and who will care for any dependents, while trusts allow you to manage and protect assets for specific purposes, like a child's education or future needs. Make sure these documents reflect your current family situation, especially after major changes such as the birth of a child, marriage, or adoption.

Designate guardians for your children and update beneficiaries on your retirement accounts and insurance policies. Working with an estate planner can simplify this process and provide peace of mind, ensuring your family's future is secure. Regularly reviewing your estate plan helps keep it aligned with your evolving family dynamics.

In Summary

Family financial planning in your thirties is about balancing current responsibilities with future security. By budgeting for childcare, education, and emergencies, updating insurance, and revisiting estate plans, you can build a strong financial foundation. Taking these steps now protects your family, prepares you for milestones ahead, and keeps your long-term goals, like retirement, within reach.

Health Management and Retirement Planning

Taking care of your health in your thirties is about more than just feeling good today—it's an investment in your future. Your well-being directly impacts your financial security, especially as you plan for retirement. Here's how maintaining your health now can set you up for long-term success.

Stay Active and Healthy

Regular exercise, a healthy balanced diet, and regular check-ups not only improve your quality of life but also help prevent costly chronic illnesses.

Incorporate activities you enjoy, such as jogging, biking, swimming, or yoga, into your routine to make staying active feel less like a chore and more like a habit you look forward to. Pair this with a diet rich in fruits, vegetables, lean proteins, and whole grains to fuel your body and support your overall well-being.

Taking care of your health now doesn't just pay off physically—it pays off financially, too. Preventing or managing conditions like diabetes, high blood pressure, or heart disease can reduce the need for expensive treatments, medications, and doctor visits later in life. By investing in your health today, you're not only saving money on future healthcare costs but also ensuring you have the energy, strength, and vitality to fully enjoy your retirement years.

Incorporate Health Costs into Your Budget

Health-related expenses, both routine and unexpected, should be an integral part of your financial planning. Budget for health insurance premiums, co-pays, medications, and preventive care.

If you have a high-deductible health insurance plan, consider opening a Health Savings Account (HSA). These accounts offer tax advantages and can be used for qualified medical expenses. Allocating funds for health costs ensures you're better prepared when unexpected medical bills arise, reducing financial stress.

Focus on Preventive Care

Preventive care is like your personal health insurance policy—without the fine print. Regular screenings, vaccinations, and wellness visits help catch potential health issues early, leading to quicker solutions and lower healthcare costs.

Schedule annual check-ups even if you feel perfectly fine. Early detection can save you from significant medical expenses and ensure you remain in top form to enjoy life, both now and in retirement.

Plan for Long-Term Health Costs

While retirement may seem far off, planning for potential long-term health expenses now can save you financial stress later. Costs for in-home care, assisted living, or nursing homes can be significant, so it's essential to prepare.

The best time to consider long-term care insurance is typically in your mid-fifties to early sixties, while you're still in good health, as waiting too long could result in higher premiums or even application rejection. However, it's never too early to start saving for these potential expenses. Research insurance options and create a dedicated savings fund to address future healthcare needs. Planning ahead gives you peace of mind and protects your assets in retirement.

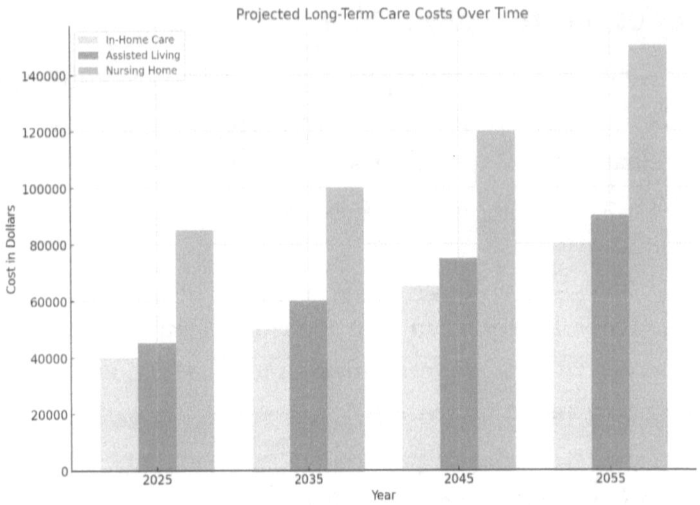

Understanding the Chart Above

The bar chart illustrates the projected costs of in-home care, assisted living, and nursing home care over the next few decades. These rising expenses highlight the importance of early planning and saving for long-term care.

Taking proactive steps now can help you avoid financial stress in retirement and ensure you have the resources to maintain your quality of life.

Avoid Unhealthy Habits

Avoiding harmful habits, such as smoking, excessive alcohol consumption, and poor eating choices, is vital for maintaining good health and managing future healthcare costs. These behaviors not only compromise your well-being but can also lead to significant medical expenses.

Focus on adopting positive lifestyle habits, and don't hesitate to seek support if you need help quitting unhealthy behaviors. Replace them with healthier alternatives that align with your goals. Surround yourself with a supportive network, and remember that small, consistent changes can lead to lasting improvements over time. Developing better health habits today means more energy, fewer health concerns, and greater freedom to enjoy life to the fullest in retirement.

ESTABLISHING AND MAINTAINING SUPPORT SYSTEMS

Building and maintaining support systems in your thirties is key to managing stress, staying motivated, and navigating life's ups and downs. These networks—whether family, friends, mentors, or professional connections—serve as your safety net and sources of inspiration. Let's explore how to effectively establish and sustain these systems for long-term benefits.

Build a Network of Professionals

A strong professional network offers valuable guidance and opportunities. Connect with mentors, industry peers, and professionals who can share their expertise and insights. Attend industry events, join professional organizations, and engage in networking activities to expand your connections.

These relationships can open doors to career advancement, business development, and personal growth. Building this network now ensures you'll have the support and resources you need as your career evolves.

Lean on Family and Friends

Family and friends are your emotional anchors. Share your goals and challenges with them and seek their advice when you need a fresh perspective. Strong relationships provide stability, encouragement, and a sense of belonging.

Regularly nurture these bonds through family gatherings, phone calls, or video chats. Even small gestures, like sending a quick text to check in, can help maintain meaningful connections and remind you of the support you have in your corner.

Engage in Community Involvement

Getting involved in your community is a great way to expand your support network while giving back. Volunteer for causes you care about and connect with others who share your passions. Community involvement fosters a sense of purpose and fulfillment while introducing you to like-minded individuals.

Whether it's joining a local club, attending neighborhood events, or taking part in a clean-up day, these activities keep you active and engaged. Bonus: you might even discover a new hobby or develop a skill along the way.

Seek Professional Advice

Sometimes, the best support comes from experts. Financial advisors, career coaches, and mental health professionals can offer tailored guidance to help you navigate complex decisions. They provide clarity, help you avoid pitfalls, and develop strategies that align with your goals.

Regular check-ins with professionals—whether it's reviewing your retirement plan, exploring a career pivot, or managing stress—ensure you stay on track and adapt to life's changes. Investing in expert guidance now pays dividends in peace of mind, stability, and confidence as you build a fulfilling future.

Cultivate Personal Interests

Engaging in hobbies and activities that bring you joy is essential. Think of it as guilt-free "me time." Personal interests, whether it's reading, painting, or learning to bake, reduce stress and enhance creativity, adding balance to your busy life.

Prioritize what makes you happy alongside your professional and family responsibilities. These moments of enjoyment contribute to a more well-rounded, satisfying life. After all, doing something purely because it brings you joy is never time wasted.

In Summary

By focusing on these strategies, you can create a strong network of support that enriches both your personal and professional life. With the right people and resources in your corner, you'll be better equipped to handle challenges, seize opportunities, and live a balanced, fulfilling life.

Balancing Present Enjoyment with Future Security

Your thirties are a decade of growth, opportunity, and discovery. You might be building a career, starting a family, or laying the foundation for stability. Amid all this progress, finding the balance between enjoying the present and planning for the future is crucial. Let's explore strategies to help you live well today while securing your tomorrow.

Set Clear Financial Goals

Define achievable financial goals that address both short-term and long-term objectives. Prioritize saving, investing, and planning for retirement. For example, aim to save a specific percentage of your income monthly, contribute consistently to your retirement accounts, and outline a strategy for reaching milestones like buying a home or paying off debt. Regularly revisit and adjust these goals to reflect your evolving priorities and financial situation.

Create a Balanced Budget

Develop a budget that balances present enjoyment with future planning. A well-crafted budget isn't restrictive—it's a tool that empowers you to live fully while preparing for what's ahead. Allocate funds for leisure activities and personal experiences that bring joy and relaxation. Whether it's a weekend getaway, a favorite hobby, or a night out, it's essential to enjoy the fruits of your hard work. At the same time, commit to saving and investing for the future. Ensure regular contributions to retirement accounts, emergency funds, and other savings goals. A balanced budget offers the peace of mind that comes from knowing you're setting yourself up to live a life that's joyful, balanced, and aligned with your values.

Plan for Major Life Events

Anticipate significant life events, such as buying a home, starting or adding to a family, or furthering your education, and include these in your financial planning. For example, if you're planning to buy a home, start saving for a down payment and related expenses like closing costs. Being proactive about upcoming milestones allows you to manage finances effectively, avoiding unnecessary stress or financial strain when these events arise.

Commit to Continuous Learning

Stay informed about financial trends, retirement strategies, and investment opportunities. The financial landscape evolves constantly, and keeping your knowledge up-to-date ensures you're making informed decisions. Read books, attend seminars, listen to podcasts, and follow trusted financial experts. Whether you're learning about shifts in the economy or exploring new investment options, continuous education empowers you to adapt and take advantage of emerging opportunities. Making learning a lifelong habit isn't just about avoiding mistakes—it's about positioning yourself to thrive in an ever-changing world.

Enjoy Life Responsibly

Find joy in life's experiences without sacrificing financial stability. It's all about balance—treat yourself to experiences that bring happiness while staying within the boundaries of your budget. For instance, splurge on an occasional concert ticket or a weekend trip, but avoid financing these pleasures with money needed for essentials. Prioritize experiences that offer genuine enrichment rather than fleeting satisfaction. Remember, fun doesn't have to break the bank. Quality time with loved ones, exploring new hobbies, or planning cost-effective adventures can provide joy and fulfillment without stretching your finances. Financial peace of mind enhances life's pleasures, making every moment sweeter.

Closing Thoughts

Your thirties are a pivotal time to balance living well today with preparing for tomorrow. By setting clear goals, creating a balanced budget, planning for major life events, and staying informed, you can build a strong foundation for a secure future. This isn't about sacrifice—it's about intentionality. Enjoy life now while confidently preparing for the retirement you deserve.

Focus on career growth, skill development, and thoughtful financial planning, all while maintaining a healthy work-life balance. The choices you make today will shape your future, paving the way for a fulfilling and prosperous retirement.

Stay purposeful, appreciate your progress, and remain committed to your goals. With intentional decisions now, you're creating a future that's secure, meaningful, and rewarding.

Resources for Further Learning

To deepen your knowledge and expand your understanding of retirement planning, career development, and financial independence, explore the following resources:

Books:

1. **"Path to Wealth: Your Road Map to Financial Independence and a Rich, Free Life"** by JL Collins - A guide to achieving financial independence through simple investment strategies.
2. **"Early Retirement Extreme: A Philosophical and Practical Guide to Financial**

Independence" by Jacob Lund Fisker - Provides unconventional strategies for achieving early retirement and financial independence.

3. **"Principles: Life and Work"** by Ray Dalio - Shares insights on personal and professional success, focusing on the principles that guided the author's journey.

Workshops and Seminars:

1. **Local Financial Planning Workshops -** Check with community centers and financial institutions for workshops on budgeting, retirement planning, and investing.
2. **Online Courses -** Platforms like Coursera, Udemy, and Khan Academy offer courses on personal finance, career development, and lifelong learning.

Professional Organizations:

1. **National Association of Personal Financial Advisors (NAPFA)** – A leading organization for fee-only financial advisors, providing access to trusted professionals who prioritize your best interests.
2. **Financial Planning Association (FPA)** – Offers resources and support for financial planners and individuals seeking financial guidance.

These resources will deepen your understanding and support your journey toward a secure and fulfilling retirement. Explore these options to gain insights, strategies, and inspiration as you build a solid foundation for your retirement and prepare for the future.

A QUICK TAKEAWAY:

Balance isn't about doing everything; it's about prioritizing what matters most.

CHAPTER THREE

MASTERING THE MONEY MOVES IN YOUR FORTIES

Embracing Midlife Growth

Whether you've successfully implemented the recommendations from earlier chapters or are just beginning your retirement planning journey, your forties are a decade filled with opportunities for growth and reflection. It's never too late to start shaping your financial future.

By now, you may have built a stable career, and your family dynamics might be shifting as your children grow, gain independence, and embark on their own journeys. If you're starting your financial planning now, don't worry—meaningful progress can still be made with focused steps.

In this chapter, we'll explore how to strengthen your financial foundation, make thoughtful mid-career adjustments, and keep your retirement planning on track. Whether you're building on existing habits or just starting out, these steps will help ensure that this stage of life is not just about maintaining what you've built, but continuing to grow toward an even brighter future.

Life in Action: Jim and Jennifer in Their Forties

Meet Jim and Jennifer, a dynamic couple in their mid-forties who showcase the power of thoughtful financial planning. Jennifer, a gifted interior decorator, thrives on transforming dull spaces into stunning masterpieces—a passion that doubles as a lucrative career. Meanwhile, Jim is a partner at a small accounting firm, where his financial expertise has been a cornerstone of their family's stability and growth.

Their journey to financial security began with a shared goal: building a solid retirement fund. They leveraged Individual Retirement Accounts (IRAs) and 401(k)s, understanding these tools as more than just accounts—they saw them as keys to a future of freedom and opportunity.

But Jim and Jennifer didn't stop at traditional retirement accounts. They expanded their portfolio by investing in real estate, purchasing two rental properties. Their plan was straightforward: pay off the mortgages, then use the properties to generate steady income in retirement. As landlords, they also valued their role in providing quality housing, contributing positively to their community.

Their financial foresight extended beyond retirement. With their oldest child heading to college in five years, they made saving for tuition a top priority. Helping their children start adulthood without overwhelming student debt was a guiding principle in their planning.

Jim also had a personal dream: early retirement. He envisioned stepping away from the demands of accounting in 15 years to savor the rewards of their hard work. This vision motivated them to maximize every financial opportunity, creating a roadmap for achieving their goals.

While their focus was on smart financial management, Jim and Jennifer were equally committed to enjoying life. They embraced their forties as a time to reassess their priorities and strengthen their financial foundation, balancing the future they were building with the present they were living.

Their days were filled with the satisfaction of progress and the joy of togetherness. Whether it was a family beach vacation, a thrilling ski trip, or a simple movie night at home, Jim and Jennifer made the most of their time. Their story captures the essence of the forties decade—a transformative period where the lessons of the past meet the opportunities of the future, creating a life that balances hard work with meaningful moments.

Welcome to Your Forties: A Decade of Purpose and Possibility

Your forties are a turning point—a time when the choices you make can profoundly shape the life you want, both now and in retirement. Think of this chapter as the next step in your story, where the wisdom you've earned meets fresh opportunities to create a life of balance, security, and fulfillment. Whether you're building on an established career or just starting to think seriously about retirement, this is your moment to take meaningful action. Let's dive into strategies that will help you grow, save, and thrive in this exciting stage of life.

Mid-Career Reflection and Career Advancement

Take a deep breath and reflect on where you are. Are you doing work that excites you? Whether you're climbing the corporate ladder, running your own business, or thriving in a skilled trade like plumbing, carpentry, or electrical work, this is the decade to explore opportunities that bring both personal satisfaction and financial stability.

Consider investing in yourself through further education, certifications, or training programs. These efforts can lead to promotions, higher-paying roles, or even a career pivot into something you're passionate about. Increasing your earning potential now not only enhances your day-to-day life but also allows you to supercharge your retirement savings for the future you're building.

Maximizing Retirement Contributions

Your forties are the perfect time to prioritize your retirement savings. If you haven't already, start contributing the maximum to your IRAs and workplace retirement plans. Take full advantage of employer matches—they're free money!

Aim to save 15–20% of your income for retirement. While catch-up contributions kick in at age 50, planning for them now sets you up for a seamless transition into the next phase of savings. Think of every dollar you save today as a gift to your future self—one that brings you closer to financial independence and peace of mind.

Proactive Debt Management and Investment Diversification

Debt can feel like a heavy weight, but your forties are the time to start lightening the load. Tackle high-interest debts first, like credit cards, to free up cash for saving and investing. Start with smaller balances for a quick win, then tackle larger debts like student loans or mortgages.

Once your debts are manageable, turn your attention to growing your wealth. Diversify your investments to balance security with growth potential. Blend lower-risk options, such as Certificates of Deposit (CDs) or Treasury bonds, with growth-oriented assets like stocks or mutual funds. Regularly review your portfolio to ensure it reflects your financial goals, comfort level, and timeline. Consulting with a financial advisor can help you strike the right balance and stay on track.

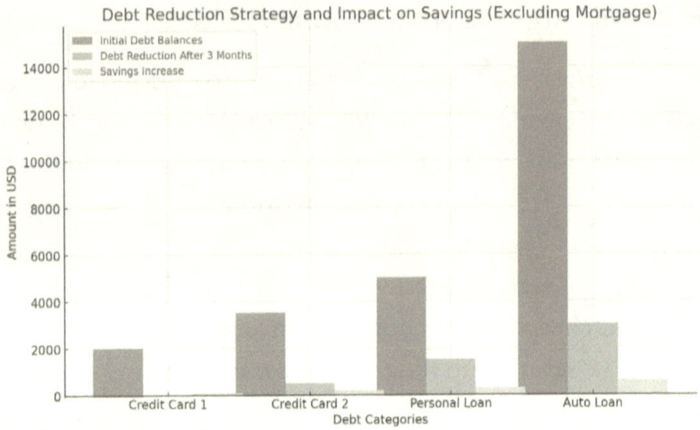

Understanding the Chart Above

This bar chart illustrates the benefits of prioritizing debt reduction, focusing on high-interest liabilities like credit cards and personal loans. By reducing these debts, you free up resources that can be redirected into savings, creating a stronger financial foundation.

This approach not only alleviates financial stress but also accelerates your ability to invest in long-term goals, such as retirement or emergency funds. Strategic debt reduction is a powerful tool for achieving financial stability as you approach your fifties.

Reassessing Financial Goals and Building Resilience

Life changes, and so should your financial goals. Take time to reevaluate your priorities and adjust your plans as needed. Look closely at your assets, debts, income, and savings to identify areas for improvement and ensure your goals align with your evolving needs.

Consider adding a safety net by exploring additional income streams. Whether it's starting a side business, investing in real estate, or pursuing freelance work, having multiple income sources can protect you against unexpected challenges. Building financial resilience means creating a life where surprises don't derail your stability.

Setting Retirement Milestones and Staying Flexible

Break your retirement journey into achievable milestones. Whether it's paying off high-interest debt, fully funding your emergency savings, or hitting a specific retirement savings target, these goals will give you clear markers of progress and keep you motivated.

At the same time, stay adaptable. Life has a way of throwing curveballs—whether it's changes in your health, career, or family dynamics. Revisiting your retirement plan regularly ensures it aligns with your current circumstances. It's important to understand that you don't need to figure all this out on your own. Help is available, and working with a financial advisor can provide guidance, clarity, and confidence as you navigate these changes and move forward.

In Summary

Your forties are a powerful blend of reflection and action. By embracing mid-career growth, prioritizing savings, and building financial resilience, you're not just planning for a better retirement—you're creating a secure, meaningful life today. This is your time to focus on what truly matters, take control of your future, and build a foundation for years filled with purpose, growth, and strength. Let's make this decade count!

INFLATION AND UNEXPECTED FINANCIAL RISKS

As you move through your forties, building your retirement accounts and reaching financial milestones might feel like the main objectives. However, two often-overlooked factors can quietly undermine your careful planning: inflation and unexpected financial risks. Addressing these challenges is just as essential as contributing to your retirement accounts.

Inflation's Silent Erosion of Wealth

Inflation is often called the "silent thief" because it gradually reduces the purchasing power of your money. As the cost of goods and services rises, the nest egg you've worked so hard to build may not stretch as far as you expect in retirement.

For example, a retirement budget based on today's prices might fall short in 15 or 20 years, when healthcare, housing, and other living expenses have increased. To guard against inflation:

Consider Inflation-Protected Investments: Treasury Inflation-Protected Securities (TIPS) are a solid option, as they adjust with inflation to help your savings retain value.

Diversify Your Portfolio: Investments that grow with inflation, such as real estate or dividend-paying stocks, can bolster your purchasing power over time.

Taking these steps now will better equip you to maintain a comfortable lifestyle in retirement, even as the cost of living rises.

Preparing for Financial Curveballs

Beyond inflation, unexpected financial risks—like economic downturns, health crises, or family emergencies—can disrupt even the most thoughtful plans. While these scenarios can be uncomfortable to think about, preparing for them offers peace of mind and financial flexibility.

Build a Solid Emergency Fund: Aim to save at least six months' worth of living expenses to cover unforeseen costs, such as job loss, medical bills, or major home repairs. This fund allows you to handle surprises without dipping into your retirement savings.

Strengthen Insurance Coverage: Policies like long-term care insurance, life insurance, and umbrella insurance can provide protection against large, unexpected expenses. Consulting with a financial advisor or insurance specialist ensures you select the right coverage for your needs.

Flexible Tools for Financial Resilience

Consider incorporating hybrid financial tools into your retirement strategy to manage unexpected expenses:

Annuities: These provide a guaranteed income stream, regardless of market conditions, offering stability in uncertain times.

Home Equity Lines of Credit (HELOCs): These can serve as a backup source of funds during emergencies. However, it's essential to weigh the risks and benefits, as improper use of these tools could impact your long-term financial security.

In Summary

By proactively addressing inflation and preparing for unexpected financial challenges, you're not just planning for retirement—you're safeguarding your future. This approach ensures that your hard work remains protected and your financial stability stays intact, no matter what life throws your way.

Career Longevity and Skill Relevance

As you move through your forties, your career path might feel well-established, but in today's rapidly evolving economy, staying relevant is more important than ever. While your twenties and thirties were focused on building a foundation, your forties are about protecting and future-proofing your career. Keeping your skills sharp and adapting to new opportunities will help you remain competitive and ensure a smoother transition into retirement.

Staying Competitive in an Evolving Workforce

The workforce is constantly changing, driven by technological advancements and industry shifts. Automation, AI, and other innovations are reshaping roles across all sectors. Ask yourself, "Will the skills I have today still be in demand 10 years from now?"

One effective way to stay competitive is through upskilling—learning new skills or enhancing existing ones to meet current demands or prepare for future opportunities. Consider options like:

- Taking online courses to master emerging technologies or tools.
- Earning certifications to stay current with industry standards.
- Pursuing advanced degrees or specialized training.

Platforms like Coursera, LinkedIn Learning, and industry-specific certification programs can help you stay ahead of the curve. Even if these skills aren't immediately needed, having them will make you a more adaptable and valuable professional. This adaptability ensures you're ready to transition into new roles or industries if necessary.

Planning for a Partial Retirement

Phasing into retirement, rather than stopping work entirely, is becoming a popular choice. Many prefer to ease into this stage through part-time work, consulting, or freelancing—either for financial stability or because they enjoy working.

Consider how your current skills and experience could translate into part-time roles or consulting opportunities in the future. Possibilities include:

- Taking on advisory roles.
- Mentoring younger colleagues.
- Consulting on projects where your expertise adds value.

This approach provides supplemental income and keeps you mentally and socially engaged in your later years. Starting to think about this phase now can give you a head start in shaping how you'd like your semi-retirement to look.

Exploring New Career Opportunities

Your forties might also be the ideal time to pivot into a new career altogether. If your current industry shows signs of slowing down, or if you're ready for a change, consider exploring new paths.

Taking calculated risks and pursuing fields you've always been interested in could open doors to greater satisfaction and security. By making these adjustments now, you'll position yourself for long-term career longevity, whether through new roles, industries, or business ventures.

Thriving in an Adaptable Career

Keeping your skills relevant and your career adaptable isn't just about staying employed—it's about thriving and preparing for a fulfilling retirement. By investing in yourself today, you take control of your work-life balance and career trajectory, ensuring you have the flexibility to decide when—and how—you'd like to retire.

Adjusting to the Empty Nest and Strengthening Relationships

Navigating your forties can feel like stepping into uncharted territory, especially as your kids grow up and leave the nest. If you started your family later, you might not experience this phase until you're in your fifties. Whenever it happens, this stage is less about missing your kids and more about adjusting to the newfound quiet in your home. But there's a silver lining: this extra space can be a blank canvas for creating a fulfilling midlife chapter.

Review Household Expenses

With fewer mouths to feed and fewer daily expenses, now is an ideal time to reevaluate your household budget. Consider how you can redirect extra funds toward financial goals like increasing your retirement savings or paying off debt. However, keep in mind the potential costs of supporting your children during their college years. Planning ahead ensures you can provide assistance while staying on track with your financial stability.

Financially Support Your Children

Reassess the level of financial support you're providing to your children and make sure it aligns with your retirement goals. Open communication is key—have honest discussions about your financial situation and encourage your kids to take steps toward independence, such as applying for scholarships or taking on part-time jobs. This helps balance their needs with your long-term financial security.

Reconnect with Your Spouse

Use this phase to nurture your relationship and plan for the future together. Dedicate quality time to each other through date nights, shared goals, or exploring new activities. Whether it's picking up a hobby as a couple or rediscovering the joy of simply spending time together, this is your chance to deepen your connection and reignite the spark in your marriage.

Travel and Pursue Hobbies

With fewer family responsibilities, embrace this newfound freedom to pursue hobbies and adventures that bring you joy. Revisit your travel bucket list or dive into passions like learning a language, painting, or even something unique like synchronized swimming. This is your opportunity to focus on personal growth, create lasting memories, and enjoy life on your own terms.

A Fresh Opportunity

Empty nest syndrome isn't just about a quieter house—it's a fresh chapter for personal growth, financial recalibration, and rekindling relationships. Embrace this stage with enthusiasm and focus on the exciting possibilities ahead. Life's too short not to enjoy a well-planned retirement and, who knows, maybe even a few synchronized swimming trophies on the shelf.

Nurturing Passions and Hobbies in Your Forties

Your forties are like a treasure chest waiting to be opened—a perfect time to dive into activities that bring joy and meaning to your life. This decade offers opportunities to discover or deepen passions, foster creativity, and enhance personal fulfillment. Let's explore how nurturing your hobbies and interests can make this chapter of life even more rewarding.

Discovering Your Spark

Think of your forties as the ultimate playground for exploration. Whether you're learning something new online, diving into a creative pursuit, focusing on your health, or brainstorming business ideas, this is your time to find what lights you up.

It's not just about having fun—it's about discovering what energizes you and makes this decade uniquely yours. Take the leap into activities that feel exciting and meaningful.

Cultivate Lifelong Learning

Lifelong learning enriches your mind and opens doors to new opportunities. Take online courses, attend workshops, or join community classes that align with your interests.

Expanding your skills can lead to personal growth and even new ventures. Whether you're exploring a new language, learning to code, or brushing up on photography, every step enhances your future while keeping your mind engaged.

Pursue Creative Outlets

Creative pursuits like blogging, painting, or even starting a small business can bring personal fulfillment and, potentially, financial benefits. Use your hobbies to express yourself or turn them into opportunities to earn supplemental income.

For example, consider building a website to promote or sell your creative work, whether it's art, writing, or handmade goods. You never know where these passions might lead until you take the first step.

Prioritize Health and Wellness Activities

Invest in your health with activities like yoga, hiking, or a gym membership. Staying active now not only enhances your quality of life but also prepares you for a healthier and more active retirement.

Incorporating regular exercise and mindfulness practices can improve physical health, mental clarity, and emotional resilience. Make your well-being a priority—it's an investment with lifelong returns.

Explore Entrepreneurial Ventures

If you've ever dreamed of starting your own business, now might be the perfect time. Consider entrepreneurial opportunities tied to your passions, much like Jennifer envisioned a boutique tied to her interior decorating.

Starting a venture that resonates with your skills and interests can provide purpose, fulfillment, and even financial rewards. Whether it's consulting, crafting, or launching a niche product, explore the possibilities that excite you.

Engage in Networking and Social Activities

Join local hobby groups or online communities to connect with people who share your interests. Networking with like-minded individuals can enrich your social life and create opportunities for collaboration or joint ventures.

Engaging with these communities expands your personal and professional circles, offering inspiration and potential partnerships. You never know what opportunities may arise when you put yourself out there.

Building a Future of Fulfillment

Investing time in your hobbies isn't just about the present—it's about planting seeds for a fulfilling future. Your passions today will continue to bring joy and purpose as you approach retirement. Your forties are like a great story—each chapter gets better, especially when it's filled with activities that truly make you happy.

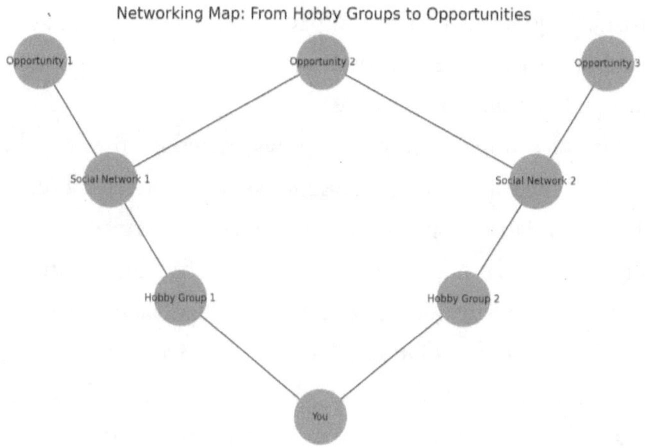

Understanding the Map Above: This networking map demonstrates how joining hobby groups and social communities can lead to new opportunities and connections. Engaging with these groups expands your social circle, introduces you to like-minded individuals, and can lead to exciting collaborations, job offers, or ventures.

This visual emphasizes the importance of finding and engaging with communities aligned with your interests. These connections are about more than just socializing; they're about opening doors to possibilities that can enrich both your personal and professional life.

Closing Thoughts

Your forties are about much more than crunching numbers—they're about creating a solid foundation for the future you've always envisioned. Every financial decision, career adjustment, and personal choice you make today helps shape the retirement you desire.

In this chapter, we explored strategies for strengthening your financial footing, including reassessing your career, managing debt, and increasing retirement contributions. We also emphasized the importance of setting clear goals and staying adaptable as life evolves.

The decisions you make now—whether they're about advancing your career, making smarter investments, or nurturing relationships—will have a lasting impact on your ability to achieve a secure, balanced, and fulfilling retirement. This is your opportunity to solidify your financial position while setting the stage for a life filled with purpose and stability.

By planning carefully and staying flexible, you can enjoy peace of mind knowing you're on the right path toward a rewarding retirement journey.

For more insights and actionable steps, explore my books *Rise Above the Rut* and *Small Changes, Big Results*. These resources offer practical advice to help you stay motivated and focused during this pivotal decade and beyond.

Here's to making the most of your forties and moving confidently toward your retirement goals!

Resources for Further Learning

To deepen your understanding of navigating your forties, mid-career adjustments, financial planning, and maintaining a fulfilling life balance, consider exploring these resources:

Books:

1. **"The Next Millionaire Next Door: Enduring Strategies for Building Wealth"** by Thomas J. Stanley and Sarah Stanley Fallaw - Explores habits and strategies that have helped everyday Americans accumulate wealth, focusing on practical approaches to financial independence.
2. **"Your Money or Your Life: 9 Steps to Transforming Your Relationship with Money and Achieving Financial Independence"** by Vicki Robin and Joe Dominguez - A comprehensive guide on how to achieve financial independence through mindfulness, frugality, and intentional living.
3. **"The Psychology of Money: Timeless Lessons on Wealth, Greed, and Happiness"** by Morgan Housel - Offers insights into how emotions and personal experiences shape our financial decisions and how to manage money more wisely.

Workshops and Seminars:

1. **Local Career Development Workshops -** Check with local community colleges, libraries, or career centers for workshops focused on mid-career advancement, job search strategies, and skill development in your forties.
2. **Estate Planning Seminars -** Many financial institutions and legal offices offer free or low-cost seminars on estate planning, an important consideration as you approach midlife.

3. **Financial Wellness Programs** - Some employers offer financial wellness programs, including seminars on retirement planning and debt management, which can be especially useful in your forties.

Professional Organizations:

1. **American Association of Retired Persons (AARP)** - Offers a wealth of resources for individuals in their forties and beyond, including financial planning tools, career resources, and lifestyle advice. Visit aarp.org for more information.
2. **Certified Financial Planner Board of Standards (CFP Board)** - Provides a directory of certified financial planners and educational resources to help you make informed financial decisions in midlife. Explore more at cfp.net.
3. **Encore.org** - Focuses on second careers and meaningful work in the later stages of life, providing resources and support for those seeking to make a career shift in their forties and fifties.

These resources will help you expand your knowledge and enhance your approach to financial and career planning in your forties. Explore these tools to gain insights, strategies, and inspiration as you navigate this pivotal decade and build a secure, fulfilling future.

A QUICK TAKEAWAY:

Success in retirement comes from balancing planning, purpose, and flexibility along the way.

CHAPTER FOUR

POWERING UP YOUR FIFTIES

Evolving with Purpose

Your fifties are more than just a milestone—they're a turning point, full of opportunities to reflect on your journey so far and lay the groundwork for the retirement you've been dreaming about. This is your chance to use your hard-earned wisdom, career experience, and support system to take meaningful steps toward the next exciting chapter of your life.

In this chapter, we'll focus on making the most of this important decade. Together, we'll answer key questions like: What's your ideal retirement age? How can you make the most of your retirement accounts and maximize Social Security benefits? And what steps will help you feel confident and prepared as you approach retirement?

To bring these ideas to life, we'll follow Margie's story—a real-life example of someone navigating the ups and downs of her fifties with purpose and determination. Her experiences will offer practical insights and lessons you can apply to your own journey.

Let's dive in and make your fifties the starting point for an exciting and well-planned retirement. You've got this!

Life in Action: Margie in Her Fifties

Margie's fifties brought her to a turning point. Three years after her divorce, she was cautiously venturing back into the dating world. The thought of committing to a new relationship felt overwhelming, but the loneliness she occasionally felt reminded her that she wasn't ready to give up on companionship.

Her son, Steve, had recently graduated from college and moved to another state for work. Margie was immensely proud of his success, but his departure left a noticeable quiet in the home she had worked so hard to maintain. As a dedicated veterinarian, Margie had built a stable career, but her finances weren't exactly where she wanted them to be. Supporting Steve's education had been a priority, and she had dipped into her retirement savings to help him graduate debt-free. Now, she was eager to rebuild her financial foundation.

Selling her family home—a place rich with memories—was a bittersweet but practical decision. With ten years left on the mortgage, along with steep taxes and maintenance costs, downsizing was the logical choice for securing her financial future. Her plan was to work another decade, putting herself in a strong position to retire comfortably.

Margie had always dreamed of traveling, envisioning trips with friends or joining group tours to explore destinations she had only seen in pictures. With her car fully paid off and her credit card debt under control, she was optimistic about making this dream a reality. However, she felt unsteady when it came to investments and budgeting, as her ex-husband had managed those areas during their marriage.

Margie's story is a reminder that the fifties can be a time of reinvention, filled with challenges but also opportunities to rediscover passions, set new goals, and regain control over your financial and personal life.

Retirement Timing

Deciding when to retire isn't just about picking a date—it's about setting the stage for the life you envision. Whether you're eager to travel the world, dedicate time to a passion, or simply enjoy a slower pace, your retirement timing shapes your financial strategy and overall experience. Here are some key factors to consider:

Embrace Change

Retirement plans aren't set in stone. For example, if you originally aimed to retire at 65 but an opportunity arises earlier, such as a volunteer position at a local animal shelter, you might choose to retire sooner to pursue that passion. Flexibility is key in making your retirement feel fulfilling and aligned with your goals.

Financial Goals

Your dreams play a big role in determining when you can retire. If you hope to travel extensively, you may need to save more, potentially delaying your retirement. Conversely, if staying physically active is your priority, retiring earlier could allow you to enjoy those adventures while you're at your healthiest.

Seek Professional Guidance

A financial advisor can help you navigate the complexities of retirement timing. They can evaluate the impact of retirement at various ages based on your savings and suggest strategies to help you achieve your goals more efficiently. Professional advice ensures you're making informed choices, balancing aspirations with financial readiness.

Retirement isn't an all-or-nothing decision. Think of it as a flexible process, where timing your transition allows you to make the most of your circumstances.

A Gradual Path to Retirement

For example, I chose a gradual retirement. At age 65, I transitioned from full-time management to working part-time—two days a week for two years, then one day a week for three more years. Now, I work PRN, picking up shifts when it suits my schedule. This phased approach let me maintain an income while enjoying more time for leisure and personal growth.

Retirement is deeply personal. Set your own pace and take it step by step. Each decision shapes your financial future and lifestyle, helping you strike the balance that works best for you.

Balanced Asset Allocation Strategy for Someone in Their 50s

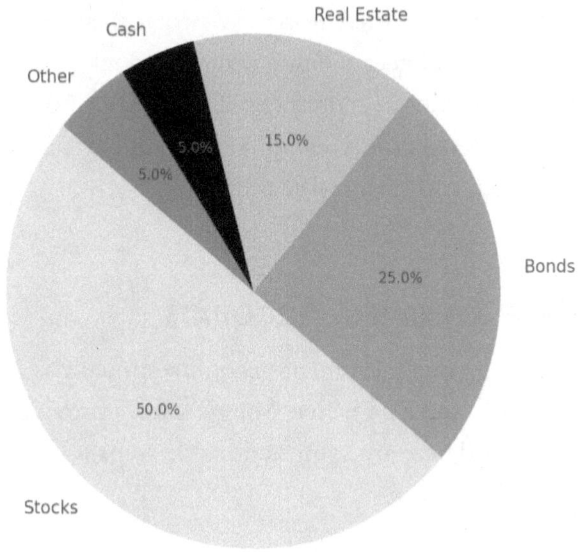

Understanding the Chart Above

The accompanying pie chart illustrates a typical asset allocation strategy for someone in their fifties, balancing stocks, bonds, real estate, cash, and other investments. A diversified portfolio helps minimize risk while allowing for steady growth—essential as you approach retirement.

Balancing Risk and Growth

While it's tempting to shift entirely to low-risk assets like bonds or cash as retirement nears, maintaining some growth-oriented investments, like stocks, is important to outpace inflation. Striking the right balance ensures your savings continue to grow while reducing exposure to market volatility.

A well-diversified portfolio protects against financial downturns and keeps your savings on track to support you through decades of retirement. This balance provides peace of mind, enabling you to enjoy your retirement with confidence and financial security.

Review Retirement Accounts

Reviewing your retirement accounts annually is like giving your future self a high-five. Margie's story provides valuable lessons, and here are some actionable steps to enhance your financial position:

Maximize Contributions

In your fifties, it's the perfect time to ramp up 401(k) contributions to make up for lost time. Adding extra dollars to a Roth IRA can also be a smart move—who doesn't love tax-free withdrawals in retirement?

With many earlier financial obligations behind you, this decade is your chance to turbocharge retirement savings. As we discussed in the chapter on your forties, you become eligible to begin catch-up contributions at age 50. Use these additional savings opportunities to take full advantage of this critical time.

Asset Allocation and Diversification

As retirement approaches, consider a more cautious investment strategy. Find the right mix of stocks, bonds, real estate, and other assets to reduce risk while still allowing for growth. As shown in the chart above, a balanced asset allocation is essential for managing market fluctuations.

Diversification acts as your financial safety net, shielding your portfolio from major swings while offering steady growth potential. Regularly reassess your investments to ensure they align with your risk tolerance and retirement timeline.

Review Retirement Income

Try a test run of your retirement income to preview your future finances and identify any gaps in your budget.

- **Calculate Expected Income**: Add up monthly income from sources like Social Security, pensions, and investments.
- **Simulate Retirement Spending**: Set aside current income and live only on your projected retirement income for a few months.

- **Track Expenses**: Ensure your budget covers housing, utilities, healthcare, groceries, entertainment, and extras.

This exercise helps spot areas where adjustments are needed, like trimming expenses or boosting savings. It can also uncover overlooked costs, such as unexpected medical bills or home repairs, giving you time to address them before retirement.

Consider Professional Advice

If navigating the financial landscape feels overwhelming, consider seeking guidance from a retirement-focused financial advisor.

Think of a financial advisor as your financial GPS—offering tailored advice on managing funds, adjusting investments, and staying on course. Just as a GPS saves time and prevents wrong turns, an advisor helps you avoid costly mistakes and ensures your retirement plan remains on track.

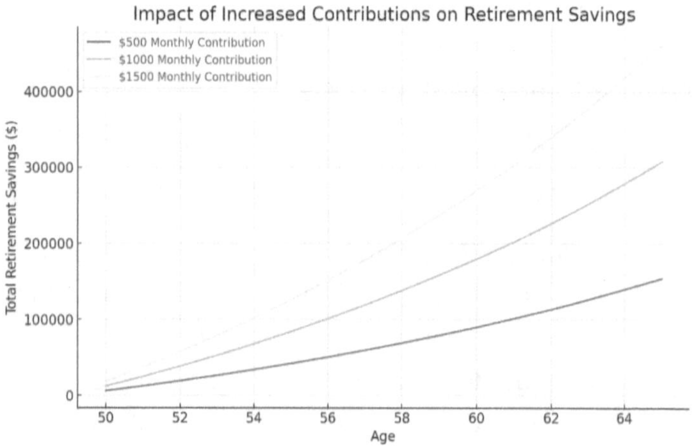

Understanding the Chart Above

This chart illustrates how different monthly contribution amounts—$500, $1,000, and $1,500—can grow your retirement savings from age 50 to 65, assuming a 6% annual return. It showcases the power of compound interest and highlights how catch-up contributions in your fifties can significantly boost your retirement nest egg.

The more you contribute now, the stronger your financial foundation will be for retirement.

In Summary

Your fifties are a vital time to refine and finalize the retirement plan you've been building. This decade provides clarity on what your retirement might look like, so embrace it as your dress rehearsal for the next exciting phase of life. Fine-tune your plan, make adjustments, and step confidently into your golden years, knowing you've done the work to create a secure and fulfilling future.

Social Security Claiming Strategies

Margie's situation as a divorced individual highlights the complexities of planning around Social Security benefits. Understanding how Social Security fits into your retirement income is crucial for making the most of your financial future. Here's how to prepare and make informed decisions about claiming Social Security:

Research and Educate Yourself

Start by learning the rules and options for claiming Social Security benefits. The U.S. Social Security Administration website (www.ssa.gov) offers detailed resources and calculators to estimate benefits at different claiming ages. Familiarize yourself with how your work history, marital status, and age impact your benefits.

Consult a Financial Advisor

Work with a qualified financial advisor who specializes in retirement planning and Social Security. They can provide personalized advice tailored to your unique situation, including your work history, marital background, and financial goals. A financial advisor can also help you evaluate how Social Security fits into your broader retirement plan.

Consider Delaying Benefits

While you can begin receiving Social Security retirement benefits as early as age 62, delaying until age 70 can significantly increase your monthly payout—by roughly 8% for each year you wait past your full retirement age.

- **Benefits of Delaying**: A higher monthly benefit can provide greater financial security during retirement.
- **Factors to Weigh**: Delaying isn't always the best choice. Consider your health, lifestyle, and immediate financial needs to determine the right claiming age for your circumstances.

Maintain Organized Records

Keep detailed records of your interactions with the SSA and any documents related to your benefits, including those involving an ex-spouse's Social Security eligibility. Organized documentation ensures a smoother application process when it's time to claim benefits.

Seek Legal Guidance if Necessary

In more complex cases, consulting an attorney may be beneficial.

- **Social Security Attorneys**: These professionals specialize in ensuring you receive the benefits you're entitled to, particularly in cases involving disputes or appeals.
- **Elder Law Attorneys**: These experts handle a wide range of issues affecting older adults, including Social Security, long-term care, and estate planning, making them ideal for navigating legal aspects of retirement benefits.

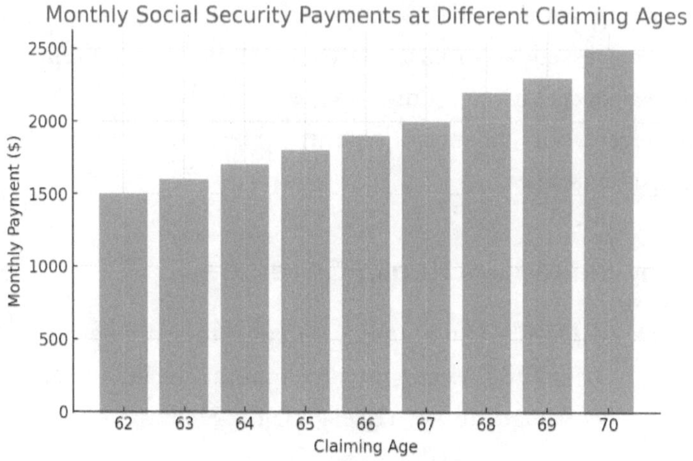

Understanding the Graph Above

The graph illustrates how monthly Social Security payments vary based on the age at which benefits are claimed, from 62 to 70. It clearly shows that delaying benefits increases your monthly payout, offering a compelling reason to wait if your financial situation allows.

By delaying until closer to age 70, you can maximize your monthly Social Security income, which can significantly impact your overall financial security in retirement.

In Summary

Taking the time to research, consult professionals, and organize your records equips you to make the best decisions regarding Social Security. Optimizing your benefits isn't just about the numbers—it's about securing your financial future and enjoying retirement with confidence.

Health Insurance and Long-Term Care Planning

Planning for health insurance and long-term care in your fifties is essential for ensuring your well-being in retirement. These decisions not only safeguard your health but also protect your financial security. Here are some key considerations:

Early Retirement Health Coverage

- **COBRA Coverage**: If you plan to retire before age 65, COBRA can provide temporary health insurance coverage until you're eligible for Medicare.

- **Spousal Coverage**: If your spouse is still working, joining their health plan could be a cost-effective option.
- **ACA Marketplace**: Explore the Affordable Care Act (ACA) Health Insurance Marketplace in your state for additional health coverage options that suit your needs and budget.

Long-Term Care Insurance

Midlife is an optimal time to evaluate long-term care insurance as part of your retirement strategy. This type of coverage can:

- **Protect Assets**: Safeguard your savings and ensure access to quality care for age-related health issues.
- **Reduce Reliance on Family**: Avoid placing the caregiving burden on loved ones or needing to qualify for Medicaid.
- **Managing Care Costs**: Help pay for in-home care, assisted living, or nursing facilities if you require help with daily activities such as bathing, dressing, or mobility.

Home Modifications

If mobility challenges arise, consider making your home more accessible. Modifications like installing handrails, ramps, or stair lifts can:

- **Enhance Safety**: Reduce the risk of falls and other accidents.
- **Support Independence**: Allow you to live comfortably in your home for as long as possible.

Health Savings Accounts (HSAs)

A Health Savings Account (HSA) offers a tax-advantaged way to save for medical expenses if you have a high-deductible health plan.

- **Lower Premiums**: Reduce current healthcare insurance costs while saving for the future.
- **Flexible Use**: Use funds for qualified expenses such as medical, dental, vision care, and prescriptions.
- **Rollover Benefits**: HSA funds roll over year to year, making them a powerful tool for covering healthcare expenses in retirement.

In Summary

Planning for healthcare and long-term care in your fifties isn't just a checklist item—it's an investment in your future peace of mind. By addressing these issues now, you'll be better equipped to enjoy your retirement without the stress of "what ifs." Taking proactive steps today ensures that you can focus on living fully and confidently in your golden years.

Debt Management

As you approach retirement, managing debt effectively becomes critical for ensuring financial stability and peace of mind. Your fifties are an ideal time to take a close look at your financial picture and develop strategies to reduce or eliminate debt, including paying off your mortgage. Entering retirement with minimal debt allows you to focus your resources on enjoying this new phase of life rather than worrying about monthly obligations.

If you have high-interest debt, such as credit card balances, it's important to prioritize paying those off first. These types of debt often come with high financial strain, as interest accrues quickly and can eat into your savings. Start by creating a structured debt repayment plan. Focus on the debts with the highest interest rates while making minimum payments on others. This targeted approach not only reduces the burden of high-interest debt but also frees up more resources for your retirement savings.

For those feeling overwhelmed or unsure about the best way to tackle their debts, seeking financial counseling can be a game-changer. A financial counselor can provide tailored advice and actionable steps to help you navigate your unique situation. Their expertise can give you clarity and confidence as you work toward a debt-free retirement.

Another key consideration in your fifties is your mortgage. Evaluate whether it's feasible to pay it off before retirement. Eliminating a mortgage payment can significantly reduce your monthly expenses and provide greater financial flexibility. If paying off your mortgage isn't realistic, consider other options, such as refinancing to lower your monthly payments or adjusting your budget to ensure the remaining payments are manageable alongside other retirement expenses.

In Summary

By focusing on debt reduction during your fifties, you can enter retirement on solid financial footing. Prioritizing high-interest debts, seeking professional guidance when needed, and evaluating your mortgage options are all effective steps to strengthen your financial security. This decade offers a valuable opportunity to set yourself up for a more relaxed and enjoyable retirement, free from the stress of lingering debt.

Maintaining Physical and Mental Health

In In your fifties, prioritizing your physical and mental well-being is just as essential as planning for a financially secure and fulfilling future.

If you haven't already, this is the time to adopt habits that will keep you active, sharp, and ready to enjoy the years ahead. By focusing on your well-being now, you'll set yourself up for a retirement filled with vitality, balance, and readiness to embrace new opportunities.

Start with regular check-ups. Scheduling annual visits with your healthcare provider allows you to monitor your health, catch potential issues early, and discuss preventive strategies tailored to your needs. These visits are like a tune-up for your body, ensuring everything is running smoothly as you prepare for the next phase of life.

Physical activity is another cornerstone of staying healthy. Joining a local hiking or walking club is a great way to stay fit while enjoying social interaction and the beauty of nature. For those who prefer working out at home, investing in equipment like a Peloton or NordicTrack can make it easier to maintain an active lifestyle. The key is finding activities you enjoy so you'll stick with them.

Your diet plays a significant role in your overall health. Growing a vegetable garden, for instance, not only provides a steady supply of fresh, delicious produce but also encourages a more nutritious diet. There's nothing quite like the satisfaction of eating tomatoes you've grown yourself, even if you have to return to store-bought during the off-season. A balanced diet full of fruits, vegetables, whole grains, and lean proteins can make a world of difference in how you feel now and as you age.

Don't overlook mental well-being. Practicing mindful meditation can help you manage stress and maintain a positive outlook, especially during life's transitions. Mindfulness isn't just a trendy concept—it's a practical tool for navigating challenges and staying grounded. For more tips on mindfulness, Chapter Three of my book *Rise Above the Rut* offers helpful guidance.

Finally, prioritize your sleep. Establishing a relaxing bedtime routine and sticking to a consistent sleep schedule ensures you're well-rested and ready to tackle each day. Quality sleep supports your physical health, mental clarity, and emotional resilience—essential components of a well-rounded, healthy lifestyle.

In Summary

By focusing on these areas—regular check-ups, physical activity, a balanced diet, mindfulness, and consistent sleep—you're building a foundation for lasting health and well-being. These habits will not only prepare you for a vibrant retirement but also help you enjoy life to its fullest right now. Small, consistent actions today will pay off in a fulfilling and energetic future.

Strengthening Relationships and Social Connections

Your fifties are an ideal time to focus on strengthening relationships and building new connections. By nurturing family bonds, deepening friendships, and engaging with your community, you can ensure that your social network continues to grow and thrive as you approach retirement. These connections are essential for maintaining emotional well-being and a sense of purpose.

If you have children or close friends living far away, make it a priority to stay connected. Schedule regular video calls to maintain a sense of closeness, even across distances. When possible, plan visits to spend quality, in-person time together. These efforts help ensure that physical distance doesn't weaken the emotional bonds that matter most.

Expanding your social circle is another way to stay connected and engaged. Joining groups or clubs centered around your interests—such as a local book club, hiking group, or gardening club—can introduce you to others who share your passions. Shared activities often form the foundation of strong, lasting friendships, whether your interests include knitting, competitive board games, or something entirely unique.

Community engagement is another valuable avenue for connection. Volunteering allows you to deepen your ties to the community while giving back in meaningful ways. Look for opportunities that align with your passions, such as helping out at an animal rescue, tutoring students, or working in a community garden. Not only will you meet like-minded individuals, but volunteering also brings a sense of purpose and fulfillment to your daily life.

By prioritizing family bonds, expanding your social circle, and engaging with your community, you're creating a strong support system for the future. These connections will bring joy, belonging, and emotional resilience as you transition into retirement. Investing in relationships now ensures a more meaningful and rewarding life in the years to come.

Discover New Passions and Hobbies

Your fifties are about more than just counting the days until retirement—it's about embracing opportunities to discover new interests and explore activities that ignite your enthusiasm. Whether it's learning a new skill, expressing your creativity, or diving into a business venture, this is the perfect time to cultivate passions that enrich both your present and future.

Lifelong learning is a fantastic way to expand your horizons. Enrolling in online courses can open up opportunities to explore new interests. For example, learning a new language could set the stage for more meaningful travel experiences, allowing you to connect with locals in a deeper, more personal way. Alternatively, diving into a subject that fascinates you—whether it's history, art, or technology—can add richness and depth to your understanding of the world.

Creative outlets like photography offer another avenue for personal growth. Capturing beautiful moments from your travels or daily life can be both a fulfilling activity and a way to preserve cherished memories. You might consider joining a local photography class or online group to hone your skills and connect with other enthusiasts who share your passion.

Physical activities can also bring a fresh spark to your routine. Salsa dancing, for example, is not only a fun way to stay fit but also a great way to socialize and express yourself creatively. Whether it's dancing, hiking, or trying a new sport, staying active in your fifties can enhance both your physical and emotional well-being.

If you have an entrepreneurial spirit, this decade might be the perfect time to start a small online business. Consider pursuing an idea that aligns with your passions, like selling handcrafted pet accessories if you love animals. Launching a business can combine personal fulfillment with the opportunity to generate additional income, making it both a rewarding and practical endeavor.

Engaging with others who share your interests is equally important. Attending meetups, workshops, or community events can help you connect with like-minded individuals. Whether you're gathering advice for a potential business or simply expanding your social circle, these connections can inspire new ideas and create lasting relationships.

Your fifties are a prime time to enrich your life with new passions and hobbies that bring purpose and fulfillment. By pursuing activities that excite and inspire you, you'll stay mentally and physically active while laying the groundwork for a rewarding retirement. Each new endeavor adds color and meaning to your journey, making this decade not just a chapter of preparation but one of discovery and joy.

Closing Thoughts

Your fifties are a pivotal bridge to retirement, where the decisions you make now will shape the quality of your future and create the foundation for a secure and fulfilling life ahead. This is the time to focus on solidifying your financial plans, maintaining your physical and mental health, fostering meaningful relationships, and discovering new passions. Each step you take brings you closer to a retirement that's both secure and enriching.

As we transition to the next decade, when many choose to retire and finalize their plans, we'll dive into strategies for turning those plans into reality. From living your retirement dream to enjoying the rewards of your early efforts, this next chapter will guide you in making the most of the life you've worked so hard to build. Stay tuned—your best years are just around the corner.

RESOURCES FOR FURTHER LEARNING

To deepen your understanding of navigating your fifties, preparing for retirement, and maintaining both financial health and personal well-being, consider exploring the following resources:

Books:

1. **"The New Retirementality: Planning Your Life and Living Your Dreams... at Any Age You Want"** by Mitch Anthony - This book challenges traditional ideas about retirement, offering a fresh perspective on how to approach this phase of life with purpose and flexibility.
2. **"How Much Money Do I Need to Retire?"** by Todd R. Tresidder - A practical guide that breaks down the complex calculations of retirement savings into easy-to-understand concepts, helping you determine how much you need to retire comfortably.

3. **"Age-Proof: Living Longer Without Running Out of Money or Breaking a Hip"** by Jean Chatzky and Michael F. Roizen - Combines financial planning with health advice to help you live a long, financially secure, and healthy life.

Workshops and Seminars:

1. **Retirement Planning Seminars -** Many financial institutions offer free or low-cost seminars on retirement planning, specifically tailored to individuals in their fifties. Check with your local bank or financial advisor for upcoming events.
2. **Social Security Workshops -** Local community centers, libraries, or AARP often host workshops that explain the intricacies of Social Security, including when and how to claim benefits.
3. **Health and Wellness Workshops -** Look for workshops that focus on maintaining physical and mental health as you age, which can be found through local hospitals, wellness centers, or community education programs.

Professional Organizations:

1. **National Association of Personal Financial Advisors (NAPFA) -** Provides a directory of fee-only financial planners and educational resources to help you make informed decisions as you approach retirement. Visit napfa.org for more information.
2. **Society of Actuaries (SOA) -** Offers valuable research and tools on longevity, retirement risk, and

financial planning, particularly useful for those interested in understanding the long-term aspects of retirement. Explore more at soa.org.

3. **Fidelity Investments' Retirement Learning Center** - A comprehensive resource offering calculators, guides, and articles specifically designed to help you navigate retirement planning in your fifties. Visit fidelity.com/retirement to access these resources.

These resources will help you deepen your understanding and refine your approach to planning for retirement and maintaining financial and personal health in your fifties. Engage with these tools to gain insights, strategies, and inspiration as you navigate this important decade and build a secure, fulfilling future.

A QUICK TAKEAWAY:

Age is merely the number of years the world has been enjoying you. Use your fifties to give them something truly unforgettable!

CHAPTER FIVE

CROSSING THE FINISH LINE IN YOUR SIXTIES

Stepping into Retirement

The moment has arrived—retirement is no longer a distant dream; it's right in front of you! This chapter is about transitioning from planning for retirement to actually living it. Think of it like you've planned an epic road trip: the route is mapped out, the bags are packed, and now it's time to start the journey and savor every mile along the way.

To make this transition relatable, I'll share the story of Dave and Lisa, a couple who worked hard, planned smart, and are now stepping into their prime with a mix of excitement and a few jitters. Their experiences offer practical insights into navigating this new phase of life, from financial planning to embracing the freedom of retirement.

As you launch into this chapter, we'll cover essential strategies for making your money last, staying healthy, and keeping your relationships vibrant. We'll also explore ways to find purpose and fun in retirement—because this stage of life isn't just about relaxation; it's about enjoying the well-deserved rewards of your hard work. Let's get moving and get you ready to make the most of your retirement adventure.

Life in Action: Dave and Lisa's Leap into Retirement Bliss

Dave and Lisa, a couple who have spent decades building a secure future for their family, are now standing on the edge of retirement. Their story is all about hard work, shared goals, and thoughtful planning, offering some great insights for anyone preparing for this exciting chapter.

Dave, a skilled union electrician, spent 40 years in his trade, ensuring financial stability for Lisa and their three kids. His career provided for their family home, a cozy vacation cabin, and countless unforgettable family trips. After years of dedication, Dave also secured a pension that will give them steady income in retirement—a solid foundation for their financial future.

At 62, Dave has decided to retire. Family is a big reason for his choice—his father needs extra support, and he wants to spend more time with his new grandson. Still, Dave is holding off on collecting Social Security until he turns 65, so he can receive a bigger monthly payout. This decision shows how they're balancing immediate needs with long-term financial goals.

One challenge they're navigating is the healthcare gap between Dave's retirement at 62 and his eligibility for Medicare at 65. Since Lisa works part-time and doesn't have health insurance through her job, they've explored temporary options to bridge the gap. They decided to purchase a health insurance plan through the Affordable Care Act marketplace, using subsidies to lower the premium costs. Dave's pension and their savings will help cover these healthcare expenses until Medicare kicks in, ensuring they stay protected without draining their financial resources.

Their story is a powerful reminder that retirement planning goes beyond just saving money—it's about building a future where you're prepared for life's uncertainties and can embrace the opportunities ahead. It's about making thoughtful decisions, like securing healthcare coverage, balancing immediate needs with long-term goals, and staying ready for whatever comes your way. Dave and Lisa's journey shows how careful preparation and intentional choices can create a retirement that feels both secure and fulfilling, giving you the freedom to focus on what truly matters.

As we look closer at their journey, we'll explore the key steps they're taking and how you can apply them to your own retirement plans. Let's focus on the practical ways to make your transition into retirement as smooth and rewarding as possible.

REVIEW YOUR RETIREMENT TIMELINE

Planning for retirement is a major milestone, and it's all about aligning your plans with your goals and circumstances. In this section, we'll revisit some key retirement planning steps covered in earlier chapters. These highlights will act as a helpful refresher, giving you quick insights to fine-tune your final preparations. The goal isn't to offer a one-size-fits-all solution but to help you tailor your plan to your unique situation.

Define Your Retirement Date

Choosing a retirement date is one of the most important decisions you'll make. Whether you're dreaming of an early retirement or planning to stay in the workforce longer, ensure your choice aligns with your financial situation and personal commitments. If early retirement is on the table, double-check that your budget can handle it and that it fits with any family responsibilities you may have. A well-thought-out retirement date sets the tone for everything else.

Check Your Financial Readiness

Start by assessing your overall financial picture. Pensions and Social Security may provide a foundation, but your savings and investments need to bridge the gap. Estimate your expected retirement costs, including healthcare, travel, and daily living expenses, and compare these with your anticipated sources of income. If there's a shortfall, now is the time to adjust your plan. Fine-tuning your financial readiness ensures you can retire comfortably without surprises.

Social Security and Pension Benefits

Once you have a clear understanding of your overall financial picture, it's time to review all your expected sources of income, including Social Security and pension benefits. Consider whether it makes sense to claim Social Security early for immediate cash flow or to wait for a higher monthly payout. Analyze how these income streams fit into your broader financial strategy. Consulting a financial advisor can be incredibly helpful here, offering personalized guidance on timing your benefits and optimizing your retirement income for maximum impact.

Healthcare Planning

Healthcare is a critical piece of the retirement puzzle, especially if there's a gap between your retirement date and Medicare eligibility at 65. Like Dave and Lisa, who needed interim insurance, you'll need to explore your options. Review your healthcare needs and evaluate plans that fit your situation, whether through COBRA, the Affordable Care Act marketplace, or other solutions. Professional advice can clarify your options and help you make informed choices. For a deeper dive, revisit the *Empowering Your Fifties* chapter, where we explored healthcare planning in detail.

By reviewing these essential elements—your timeline, finances, benefits, and healthcare—you'll be well-equipped to step into retirement with confidence and clarity.

FINANCIAL SECURITY IN RETIREMENT

Retirement is about enjoying the life you've worked hard to build, and financial security is at the heart of that. In this section, we'll focus on strategies to make sure your money supports your retirement dreams, covering everything from investments to emergency funds.

Review Your Investment Portfolio

Start by evaluating your investment portfolio to ensure it aligns with your retirement goals. Are your investments too risky for this stage of life, or are they balanced for growth and income? Consider adding income-generating assets like dividend-paying stocks or bonds to provide steady cash flow. This is the time to fine-tune your strategy so your money works for you while minimizing unnecessary risks.

Establish a Withdrawal Plan

Having a smart withdrawal plan is essential for maintaining a steady income while minimizing taxes. Typically, the recommended approach is to withdraw from taxable accounts first, allowing tax-deferred accounts like IRAs and 401(k)s to grow longer. After that, consider withdrawing from traditional IRAs and lastly Roth IRAs, which are tax-free. A well-thought-out withdrawal strategy can balance income needs, tax obligations, and growth potential. What's your plan for turning your savings and investments into sustainable income?

Top Off Your Emergency Fund

Life is full of surprises, and an emergency fund is your financial safety net. Aim to set aside six months' worth of living expenses to cover unexpected costs like medical emergencies or home repairs. Having this cushion can provide peace of mind and protect your retirement savings from being tapped unnecessarily.

Plan for Long-Term Care

Healthcare costs, especially long-term care, can be a significant expense in retirement. Planning ahead is key. Consider long-term care insurance or other strategies to cover potential expenses like in-home care, assisted living, or nursing facilities. Preparing now helps safeguard your savings from being drained by healthcare costs later.

Eliminate Debt

Carrying debt into retirement can weigh heavily on your financial freedom. Focus on paying off high-interest debts like credit cards first, and then work on larger debts, such as your mortgage. Imagine entering retirement without monthly debt payments—your income will stretch much further, giving you greater financial flexibility and peace of mind.

Prepare for Healthcare Costs

In addition to long-term care, it's critical to review your overall healthcare expenses. We keep emphasizing healthcare coverage and costs because they are one of the top reasons many retirees face financial hardship or even bankruptcy in retirement. Explore health insurance options that cover both routine medical needs and unexpected expenses. Additionally, consider setting aside funds specifically for medical costs to provide a cushion against surprises and protect your financial stability. Proactively addressing healthcare can make all the difference in securing a stress-free retirement.

Six Practical Steps to Achieve Financial Security in Retirement

1. **Evaluate Investments**

    - **Key Question:** Do your investments align with your goals while minimizing risk and maintaining potential for future growth?
    - **Action:** Adjust your portfolio to achieve a balance between steady income and long-term growth, ensuring it reflects both your risk tolerance and financial objectives.

2. **Create a Withdrawal Plan**

    - **Key Question:** How will you turn your savings and investments into a reliable and sustainable income stream for retirement? Have you thought about how taxes, timing, and required withdrawals will impact your strategy?

- **Action:** Develop a plan to withdraw funds in a way that supports your income needs while minimizing taxes and preserving future growth. This is a critical step to ensure your savings last throughout retirement. Seeking guidance from a financial advisor can help you create a strategy tailored to your specific goals and circumstances.

3. **Build an Emergency Fund**

   - **Key Question:** Do you have enough set aside to cover unexpected expenses, like medical bills, home repairs, or other emergencies?
   - **Action:** Strive to have at least six months' worth of essential living expenses in an easily accessible account. This fund acts as a financial safety net, providing peace of mind and helping you avoid dipping into retirement savings when unexpected costs arise. Regularly review and adjust your emergency fund to ensure it aligns with your current expenses and needs.

4. **Plan for Long-Term Care**

   - **Key Question:** How will you handle the potentially high costs of long-term care, such as in-home assistance, assisted living, or nursing facilities?

- **Action:** Think ahead and explore options to cover these expenses. This could include researching long-term care insurance, which helps protect your assets and ensures access to quality care. If insurance isn't the right fit, consider setting aside dedicated savings or building this expense into your retirement budget. Planning now reduces financial uncertainty later and ensures you're prepared for whatever healthcare needs may arise. Regularly revisiting this plan can keep it aligned with your evolving health and financial situation.

5. **Eliminate Debt**

    - **Key Question:** What's your strategy for paying off debt, and how will it impact your financial security in retirement?
    - **Action:** Prioritize clearing high-interest debts, like credit cards, which can drain your resources over time. Work on paying down larger debts, such as mortgages or student loans, to free up income and reduce financial stress before retiring. Becoming debt-free, or as close to it as possible, allows you to focus on building a sustainable retirement income without the burden of monthly payments. Regularly reassess your progress and adjust your plan to stay on track.

6. **Address Healthcare Costs**

    - **Key Question:** Are you financially prepared to manage both routine and unexpected medical expenses during retirement?
    - **Action:** Take proactive steps to secure your healthcare needs. Review your current and future insurance options, including Medicare, supplemental plans, and private insurance, to ensure they align with your anticipated medical requirements. Set aside dedicated savings to cover out-of-pocket costs, such as deductibles, prescriptions, and copayments. Healthcare can be one of the most significant expenses in retirement, so preparing now provides peace of mind and protects your financial stability. Regularly revisit your plan to adapt to any changes in health or policy coverage.

In Summary

By taking these six steps, you can build a solid financial foundation for retirement. It's not just about saving money—it's about having a plan that supports your lifestyle while accounting for the unexpected. With careful preparation and a personalized strategy, you'll be ready to embrace retirement with confidence and enjoy your hard-earned freedom without financial worries.

HEALTH AND WELLNESS IN RETIREMENT

Retirement is an incredible opportunity to prioritize your health and well-being, ensuring you have the energy and vitality to fully enjoy the years ahead. It's not just about adding years to your life—it's about adding life to your years. By focusing on physical health, mental wellness, and preventive care, you can build a retirement filled with purpose, joy, and connection.

Let's start with physical wellness. Staying active is key to maintaining your energy and overall well-being. Whether it's walking, yoga, swimming, or joining a local fitness class, regular exercise can boost your mood, keep your body strong, and improve your quality of life. It's not just about working out solo—get your spouse, family, or friends involved! Plan hikes, bike rides, or even simple morning walks together to stay motivated and accountable. Ask yourself: How can you make physical activity a regular, enjoyable part of your routine?

Mental wellness is just as important as physical health. Retirement offers the chance to nurture your mind and spirit in ways that bring fulfillment and purpose. Take up hobbies you've always wanted to try, like painting, gardening, or learning a new language. Join book clubs, volunteer for causes you're passionate about, or explore creative outlets that bring joy and keep your mind sharp. Staying socially connected is also critical. Surrounding yourself with supportive people and meaningful activities can make a world of difference. How do you plan to keep your mind engaged and your spirits high during this exciting chapter?

Finally, don't overlook the importance of preventive healthcare. Regular check-ups are your front line of defense for long-term wellness. Schedule annual physicals, dental visits, and vision screenings to catch potential health issues early. Staying proactive with your medical care helps you avoid surprises and ensures you're addressing concerns before they become bigger problems. Think about it: What's your plan for staying on top of routine medical care?

Retirement is your time to thrive, and your health is the foundation for a fulfilling future. By staying active, nurturing your mental well-being, and keeping up with preventive care, you're giving yourself the best chance to enjoy the freedom and opportunities retirement offers. Prioritizing your health doesn't mean making drastic changes overnight—it's about making thoughtful choices and sticking with habits that support your long-term well-being. The better care you take of yourself now, the more energy, joy, and peace of mind you'll have to fully embrace this exciting chapter. How will you make your health a priority?

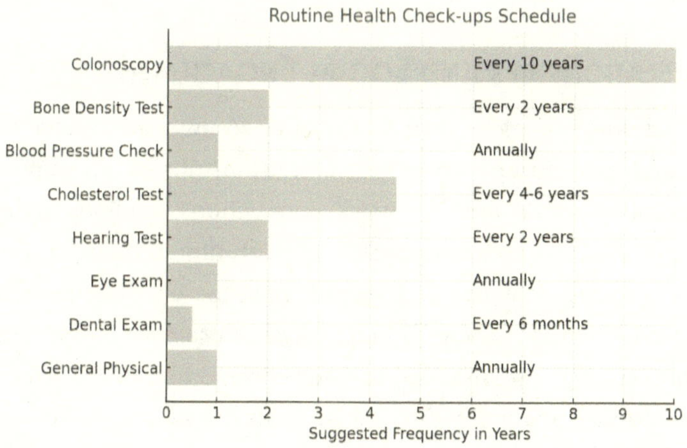

Understanding the Chart Above

The chart highlights a recommended schedule for routine health check-ups, such as annual physicals, dental cleanings, and cholesterol screenings. Following these guidelines helps detect potential issues early, ensuring proactive health management. Staying diligent with these appointments builds a strong foundation for your well-being as you age.

In Summary

Building a healthy retirement starts with physical activity, mental wellness, and regular check-ups. These steps not only sustain your health but also enhance your quality of life, ensuring you're ready to embrace retirement with vitality and confidence.

Your well-being is the cornerstone of a joyful and fulfilling retirement. By making health a priority, you're setting the stage for years of happiness and adventure ahead.

Relationships and Social Engagement

Retirement is more than financial freedom; it's a chance to build and nurture meaningful relationships and create a fulfilling social life. As work connections naturally fade, your sixties present the perfect opportunity to focus on the people and activities that matter most to you. Whether it's strengthening family bonds, deepening friendships, or becoming more involved in your community, this phase is all about enhancing your social connections and enriching your well-being.

Family Dynamics

Family plays an essential role in retirement. As dynamics shift—perhaps with the addition of grandchildren or other new family members—open communication becomes more important than ever. Plan family dinners, weekend gatherings, or group vacations to maintain strong bonds. This stage of life is also an opportunity to support and cherish your family while finding joy in evolving relationships.

Reinvent Relationships

Retirement offers a fresh start for all your relationships. If you're partnered, now is the time to discuss shared goals, make travel plans, or explore new hobbies together. Consider taking a class together, volunteering as a couple, or simply spending more quality time nurturing your bond.

If you're single, think about how you'd like to build your social life. Maybe this is the time to deepen friendships, start dating, or join community groups that align with your interests. Whether you decide to stay in your current home, move to a 55-plus community, or explore another housing option, take steps to build new connections and strengthen existing ones.

Friendships and Networking

As work-based relationships fade, maintaining friendships takes on greater importance. Rekindling old connections, joining clubs, or participating in activities you enjoy can bring both companionship and a sense of belonging. Friends can also be your partners in adventure, helping you make the most of retirement.

Expanding your social circle is equally rewarding. Volunteering, enrolling in classes, or joining community groups can introduce you to people who share your passions. These new relationships can enrich your retirement experience and provide a broader support network.

Finding Purpose in Retirement

With your daily work routine behind you, retirement is the perfect time to focus on what gives your life meaning. Purpose is about doing what feels significant to you—whether it's contributing to others, growing as a person, or simply enjoying what makes you happy. Identify your passions, interests, and goals, and use them to shape this new chapter. Whether it's mentoring, volunteering, or diving into a hobby you've always wanted to explore, now is your time to take that leap.

Consider how you'd like to make this next phase of life purposeful. Could it involve giving back to others, contributing to your community, or creating something lasting for yourself or your family? Purposeful activities not only bring fulfillment but also help you stay connected, energized, and engaged. Retirement isn't just the end of work—it's the beginning of opportunities to live a life that truly resonates with who you are.

Community Involvement

Retirement offers an opportunity to make a difference beyond your immediate circle. Volunteering at a local organization, joining clean-up efforts at parks, beaches, or neighborhoods, or even running for a local council position can be deeply rewarding. Community involvement not only lets you contribute to causes you care about but also helps you meet new people and build a broader support network.

In Summary

Retirement is the perfect time to strengthen existing relationships and create new ones. Spending quality time with family, nurturing friendships, and engaging with your community can make this chapter of life deeply fulfilling. Reach out to old friends, find new ones who share your interests, and seek out activities that bring meaning to your days.

Building a rich social life in retirement isn't just about staying busy; it's about creating a life filled with connections, experiences, and purpose. How will you make relationships and social engagement a bigger part of your retirement journey?

PURSUING PASSIONS AND HOBBIES

Retirement is the perfect time to focus on your passions and hobbies—a chance to rediscover what brings you joy and fulfillment. Whether you're eager to learn new skills, explore creative outlets, or stay active, this phase allows you to design your days around what truly matters to you.

Lifelong Learning

Keep your curiosity alive by diving into new interests and developing fresh skills. Retirement is a wonderful opportunity to explore subjects you've always wanted to learn about. Maybe you've dreamed of picking up a new language, improving your photography, or mastering woodworking. Online platforms, community colleges, and travel-based learning experiences are great ways to get started.

Specialized workshops, adult education programs, and free or low-cost classes at local libraries can also expand your horizons. Many universities and retirement communities offer programs tailored to lifelong learners. Whether you choose local or global opportunities, there's no limit to how you can continue growing and discovering.

Creative Outlets

Engage in hobbies that spark creativity and bring satisfaction. Painting, gardening, and writing are classic options, but creativity doesn't have to stop there. Practical projects like woodworking, home improvement, or cooking can be just as fulfilling.

Consider joining a local art class, taking on a DIY project, or experimenting with new recipes in a cooking class. These creative pursuits aren't just therapeutic—they add a sense of accomplishment and joy to your daily life.

Physical Activities

Staying physically active is essential for maintaining your health and energy in retirement. Explore activities you've always been curious about, like golf, dancing, or yoga. Exercise boosts physical and mental well-being, reduces stress, and keeps you feeling vibrant.

Group activities also offer the added benefit of social interaction. Whether you join a fitness class, participate in a walking club, or try ballroom dancing, staying active can make your retirement healthier and more engaging.

Entrepreneurial Ventures

If you've ever dreamed of starting a small business or researching investments, retirement can be the ideal time to make it happen. Launching a small online store, consulting, or joining a real estate partnership are just a few possibilities.

Explore resources and programs designed for retirees interested in entrepreneurship. You don't need a substantial initial investment to turn your vision into reality. Pursuing a business venture in retirement can be both financially rewarding and personally fulfilling.

Networking and Social Engagement

Retirement is the perfect time to connect with like-minded individuals and build meaningful relationships. Joining clubs, groups, or communities aligned with your passions can help you stay socially engaged and ward off boredom.

Whether it's a book club, hiking group, or local workshop, these activities foster shared experiences and valuable friendships. Who knows? You might find a new adventure partner or someone who shares your sense of humor.

In Summary

Now that you've explored the possibilities, it's time to make these ideas your own. Whether you're diving into lifelong learning, embracing creative outlets, staying active, pursuing entrepreneurial ventures, or building social connections, focus on what brings you the greatest joy and purpose.

Retirement offers the freedom to align your activities with your values and interests. By following your passions, you can craft a vibrant, fulfilling, and uniquely personal retirement. Each day is an opportunity to live fully, create lasting experiences, and make this stage of life your most rewarding yet.

Legacy Planning

As you enter your sixties, it's a meaningful time to think about the legacy you want to leave. This isn't just about financial inheritance—it's about the values, traditions, and memories you'll pass on to future generations. Legacy planning allows you to shape how you're remembered and the impact you leave behind.

Estate Planning

A solid estate plan is the foundation of legacy planning. Consult with an experienced estate planning attorney to create or update essential documents like a will, power of attorney, and trusts. These ensure that your financial and personal matters are managed according to your wishes.

Include a living will to outline your healthcare preferences and a healthcare proxy to designate someone to make medical decisions on your behalf. Don't forget to update beneficiary designations on retirement accounts and life insurance policies.

Additionally, consider your digital assets—passwords, online accounts, and social media profiles. Planning for these can simplify the process for your loved ones and provide peace of mind.

Charitable Contributions

If giving back is important to you, think about how you'd like to make a lasting impact through charitable contributions or philanthropic activities. Start by identifying causes or organizations that align with your values and passions.

You might consider setting up a charitable trust, donating to a nonprofit, or even establishing a family foundation. Research your chosen organizations to ensure your contributions are meaningful and well-directed. A thoughtful charitable giving plan allows you to support causes you care deeply about while leaving a legacy of generosity.

Passing on Traditions and Values

Legacy planning goes beyond finances. It's also about preserving and passing on the life lessons, stories, and traditions that define your family.

Consider writing a memoir or creating a family recipe book to share cherished memories. Spend time with children and grandchildren, sharing the stories and experiences that shaped your life. Reflect on what values and rituals you want future generations to carry forward, ensuring they remain a part of your family's legacy.

Planning for the Future

Think about the future you want to help create for your descendants and community. This might mean setting up educational funds for grandchildren, investing in community projects, or creating a succession plan for a family business. Your forward-thinking efforts today can provide lasting benefits for the people and causes you care about.

In Summary

Ultimately, legacy planning is about more than what happens after you're gone. It's about living intentionally now and creating a positive, lasting impact. By carefully preparing your estate, giving to meaningful causes, sharing your values, and planning for the future, you can leave a legacy that reflects who you are and the difference you want to make in the world.

Closing Thoughts

Your sixties are often a time of transition, shifting from years of planning for retirement to finally living it. It's like wrapping up a long journey and arriving at a destination you've dreamed about. This chapter explored how to align your retirement timing with your financial and personal goals, making sure you're ready to enjoy the fruits of your hard work.

We covered the essential elements of a fulfilling retirement—from achieving financial security to maintaining your health and building strong social connections. Dave and Lisa's story reminded us that thoughtful preparation creates a smoother and more enjoyable transition into this new phase of life.

As you move forward, the next chapter, *Embracing Retirement Success: The Final Checklist*, will help you navigate key milestones and ensure your retirement is everything you've envisioned. This is your moment to shine. Let's make sure every detail is in place for a retirement that's as rewarding and meaningful as you deserve. Your encore awaits—step into the spotlight and savor this well-earned stage of life!

RESOURCES FOR FURTHER LEARNING

To expand your knowledge on navigating your sixties, transitioning into retirement, and ensuring a fulfilling, financially secure life, consider exploring the following resources:

Books:

1. **"The Five Years Before You Retire: Retirement Planning When You Need It the Most"** by Emily Guy Birken - This book offers practical advice on what to do in the final stretch before retirement, covering everything from finances to lifestyle changes.
2. **"You Can Retire Sooner Than You Think: The 5 Money Secrets of the Happiest Retirees"** by Wes

Moss - Focuses on the habits and financial practices of happy retirees, providing actionable tips for achieving a joyful and secure retirement.

3. **"What the Happiest Retirees Know: 10 Habits for a Healthy, Secure, and Joyful Life"** by Wes Moss - Delivers insights on how to create a retirement filled with health, security, and happiness, based on research and interviews with successful retirees.

Workshops and Seminars:

1. **Medicare Enrollment Workshops -** Local community centers and senior services often offer workshops to help you understand your Medicare options and guide you through the enrollment process.
2. **Retirement Income Planning Seminars -** Many financial advisors and institutions host seminars focused on income planning in retirement, including how to draw down your assets effectively and tax-efficiently.
3. **Estate Planning and Legal Seminars -** Look for seminars that provide guidance on estate planning, including wills, trusts, and power of attorney, which are crucial as you finalize your retirement plans.

Professional Organizations:

1. **American Association of Retired Persons (AARP) -** A valuable resource for individuals in their sixties, offering information on retirement

planning, Medicare, and social security. Visit aarp.org for more resources.

2. **Elder Law Answers -** Provides a directory of elder law attorneys and resources on legal issues related to aging, including estate planning, Medicaid, and long-term care. Visit elderlawanswers.com.
3. **National Council on Aging (NCOA) -** Offers resources on aging well, financial security, and health management for seniors. Explore more at ncoa.org.

These resources are here to support you as you transition into retirement—whether in your sixties or whenever you choose to take the leap. They're designed to help you make informed decisions, maintain your well-being, and embrace a fulfilling and purposeful stage of life. Use these materials to deepen your understanding and make the most of your retirement years.

A QUICK TAKEAWAY:

The best is yet to come—retirement is your reward for a life well-lived

CHAPTER SIX

YOUR RETIREMENT PLAYBOOK - THE FINAL CHECKLIST

Your Journey to Retirement

Think back to your twenties, when you were just starting your career. It feels like yesterday, doesn't it? At the time, you were laying the foundation for your future—setting financial goals, forming healthy habits, advancing your career, and building a support system. You may not have realized it then, but that was the beginning of your journey toward a balanced and rewarding retirement.

In your thirties, life hit its stride. Work, family, and fun kept you busy as you focused on growing your income and making strides in your financial planning. It was a time to juggle responsibilities while still enjoying the ride.

Your forties brought refinement. Mid-career adjustments, strengthening your financial base, and perhaps tackling the empty nest phase became priorities. Even if that came with some mixed emotions, you managed to navigate these changes with resilience and determination.

As you reached your fifties and sixties, the focus shifted to fine-tuning your plans. These years were about safeguarding your finances, prioritizing your health, nurturing meaningful relationships, and creating a legacy. You also made space for what truly brings you joy—exploring passions and interests that make life fulfilling and worthwhile.

Looking back, each phase of your life has been a vital chapter in your retirement story. You've built the wisdom, support, and experiences needed to embrace retirement with confidence. This is your time—you've earned every moment of it!

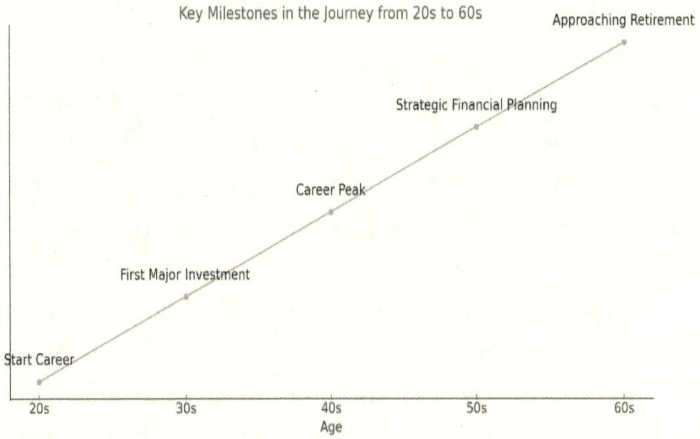

Understanding the Graph Above

The timeline graph offers a clear view of the key milestones along your journey from your twenties to your sixties. It highlights moments like starting your career, making major investments, reaching the peak of your profession, engaging in thoughtful financial planning, and approaching retirement.

By following this visual guide, you can see how each stage naturally builds on the one before it. The graph simplifies complex ideas, showing the value of long-term planning and the steady progression that leads to a successful and fulfilling life. Each step along the way contributes to the vibrant retirement you now get to enjoy.

Your Retirement is Here

Congratulations—retirement has officially arrived! But don't think of it as the end of something; it's truly the beginning of a whole new adventure. After years of hard work and dedication, this is your time to reap the rewards and fully embrace life on your own terms.

Imagine the possibilities. Whether you're traveling to bucket-list destinations, diving headfirst into new hobbies, or cherishing more time with family and friends, retirement offers the freedom to focus on what brings you the most joy. It's your life, your schedule, your rules.

You've done more than secure your finances—you've prepared holistically, considering all aspects of a fulfilling life. By prioritizing your health, nurturing relationships, pursuing passions, and focusing on emotional well-being, you've set yourself up for a retirement that truly lives up to the name "golden years."

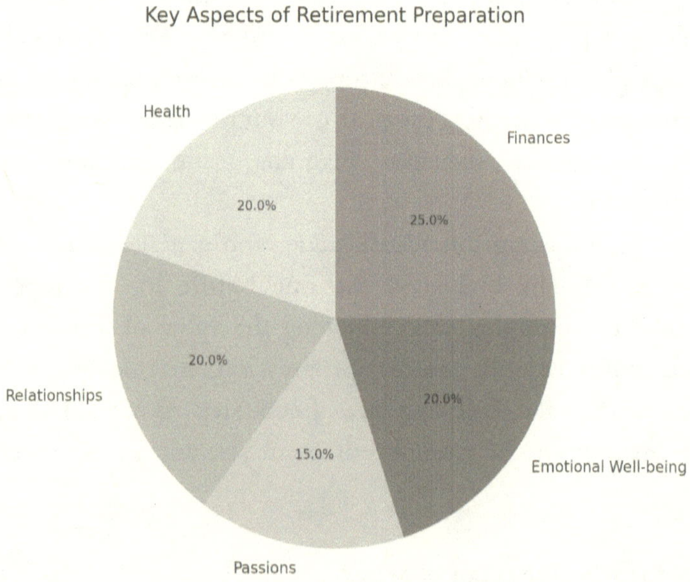

Understanding the Chart Above

This chart goes beyond financial stability to show the importance of balance across all areas of life. It emphasizes how good health, strong relationships, meaningful pursuits, and emotional wellness contribute to a truly fulfilling retirement.

Use this visual as a tool to evaluate your current plans. Are you giving enough attention to each area? If there's room for improvement, now is the time to make adjustments. Retirement isn't just about financial independence—it's about creating a well-rounded life filled with purpose, connection, and happiness.

Here's to a Bright Retirement

As you pause to reflect and prepare for this next chapter of your life, I wish you joy, health, and countless meaningful moments. Before diving into this exciting new adventure, take a moment to review this final checklist. Think of it as a quick pit stop to ensure everything is set for the retirement you've earned and deserve. Here's to celebrating this incredible milestone!

The Final Checklist

1. Review Your Retirement Timeline

- Confirm your retirement date—is it still the right fit for your goals?
- Build in flexibility—what's your backup plan if circumstances shift?

2. Secure Your Finances

- Revisit your budget—are you still on track to sustain your lifestyle?
- Review income sources like pensions, Social Security, investments, and savings to ensure they align with your needs.
- Schedule a meeting with your financial advisor to fine-tune your asset allocation.

3. Maintain Your Health and Well-Being

- Schedule health check-ups and keep up with preventive care.
- Choose the healthcare plan that offers the best coverage for your medical needs and budget.
- Establish a fitness routine—your future self will thank you!
- Maintain a healthy diet rich in fruits, vegetables, whole grains, and lean proteins to support long-term vitality.
- Prioritize mental health by staying socially connected, practicing mindfulness, and engaging in activities that bring you joy and purpose.

4. Nurture Relationships and Social Connections

- Strengthen bonds with family and friends through regular catch-ups and shared activities.
- Stay socially active by joining clubs, volunteering, or participating in community groups.
- Keep in touch with your professional network for potential opportunities and friendships.

5. Pursue Your Passions

- Revisit the hobbies or dreams you've always wanted to pursue.
- Set meaningful goals that bring purpose to your retirement.
- Enroll in classes or join groups that match your interests to stay engaged and fulfilled.
- Volunteer for causes you're passionate about to give back while doing something you love.
- Start a creative project, like writing a book, painting, or gardening, to express yourself and stay inspired.
- Mentor or share your expertise with others, whether it's through teaching, coaching, or participating in community programs.

6. Consider Your Legacy

- Update your estate plan to reflect your current wishes.
- Explore opportunities to give back through charitable donations or legacy projects.
- Have open conversations with loved ones about your plans to provide clarity and peace of mind.

7. Prepare Your Home and Living Situation

- Assess whether your current home fits your retirement plans. Do you need to downsize, relocate, or make modifications?
- Make your home a safe and comfortable space, ensuring it's easy to maintain.

- Create an environment that supports both physical and emotional well-being.

8. Financially Prepare for the Unexpected

- Ensure your emergency fund is sufficient to handle surprises like medical bills, home repairs, or unexpected travel expenses.
- Research long-term care insurance to protect your assets from potential healthcare costs.

9. Tackle Legal and Administrative Tasks

- Review and update essential documents like wills, power of attorney, and healthcare directives.
- Organize your financial and personal records for easy access.
- Share the location of these documents with trusted individuals.

10. Embrace the Freedom of Retirement

- Reflect on how you'll structure your days—what will your new routine look like?
- Stay open to new experiences, hobbies, and adventures.
- Approach this new phase with adaptability and enthusiasm.

Final Preparation Steps: Retirement Checklist

- Review Your Retirement Timeline
- Secure Your Finances
- Maintain Your Health and Well-Being
- Nurture Relationships and Social Connections
- Pursue Your Passions
- Consider Your Legacy
- Prepare Your Home and Living Situation
- Financially Prepare for the Unexpected
- Legal and Administrative Tasks
- Embrace the Freedom of Retirement

Understanding the Checklist Above

This checklist isn't just a to-do list—it's your road map to a fulfilling and secure retirement. By reviewing and addressing each step, you can feel confident that you've covered all the essential aspects, from financial security and health to social engagement, personal growth, and finding purpose. Together, these elements create a well-rounded and rewarding retirement lifestyle, ensuring this phase of life is everything you've hoped for.

Retirement is more than just a destination—it's your time to thrive. Use this guide as a tool to ensure you're fully prepared to embrace the freedom and opportunities that retirement offers. Here's to making this next chapter truly extraordinary!

Closing Thoughts

Retirement marks a milestone that reflects all the hard work, planning, and dedication you've put into building a secure future. It's not just the end of a career—it's the beginning of a chapter where you can shape your life around what truly matters. This is your time to focus on balance—between financial stability, physical and mental health, and the relationships and passions that bring you joy.

As you move forward, think of retirement as a unique opportunity to redefine your purpose. Whether it's exploring new hobbies, deepening relationships, or giving back to your community, this is your chance to create a life rich in meaning and fulfillment. Thoughtful planning has done more than prepare you financially—it has laid the groundwork for a retirement filled with experiences and possibilities that align with your values.

The beauty of retirement is that it's your journey to design. It's like stepping into a new landscape where every step you take adds to a fulfilling picture of your future. Early and intentional planning doesn't just give you peace of mind; it opens the door to a life of freedom, adventure, and purpose.

You've reached an incredible turning point, equipped with the tools to make this stage of life truly extraordinary. Here's to a retirement that's balanced, rewarding, and full of possibilities, with all the joy and adventures waiting ahead!

A QUICK TAKEAWAY:

Early planning for retirement is the key to unlocking a future full of experiences, purpose, and lasting happiness.

PART

2

CHAPTER SEVEN

WEALTH HACKS FOR EVERY STAGE OF LIFE

YOUR WEALTH-BUILDING GAME PLAN

Building wealth isn't about flashy cars or oversized homes—it's about understanding your money and making it work for you. Think of your net worth as a financial report card, showing your overall financial health. It's the total value of what you own (your assets) minus what you owe (your debts). The bigger the gap between what you earn and what you spend, the more you can save and grow your net worth over time. Remember, owning expensive things doesn't necessarily mean wealth, especially if they're financed with debt.

Get a Grip on Your Net Worth

Start by figuring out where you stand financially. Add up everything you own—cash, investments, property, and other assets—and subtract what you owe, like loans and credit card balances. This number is your net worth. Track it regularly to monitor your progress and see how your wealth grows over time.

Plan Your Financial Goals

Think of financial goals as a road trip. There are short-term stops like saving for a vacation, mid-term goals such as paying off student loans, and the ultimate destination—retirement. Online tools like Mint, Personal Capital, and Fidelity's Retirement Score can help you set and track goals, whether it's for saving, investing, or paying down debt.

Earn That Money

Your income is the fuel for building wealth, and it comes in three flavors:

- **Active Income:** This is what you earn through work—your job, side hustles, or freelance gigs. Think extra shifts, driving for Uber, or tutoring. The more you work, the more you earn.
- **Passive Income:** This includes rental properties, royalties, or investments that generate money with minimal day-to-day effort. While it takes time to set up, it's an excellent way to build long-term wealth.
- **Portfolio Income:** Income from investments like stocks, bonds, or dividends. It grows over time, especially when you reinvest your returns, which are the profits earned from your investments, such as dividends, interest, or capital gains.

Boosting income often means starting small. Consider side hustles or upskilling to increase your earning potential.

Save Money Automatically

Set up automatic transfers to your savings and retirement accounts as soon as your paycheck hits. Aim to save at least 20% of your income. If that's tough, start small and work your way up. The key is consistency.

Start Early and Let Time Work for You

The earlier you start saving and investing, the more time your money has to grow through the power of compound interest. For example, investing $5,000 a year starting at age 25 could grow to over $1 million by age 65, assuming a 7% average annual return. However, if you wait until age 35 to start, that same investment will grow to only about half that amount by age 65. Time is your greatest asset—don't let it slip away. Start now and let your money work for you.

Invest Smartly

Don't let all your money sit idle in a low-interest savings account. Diversify your investments across stocks, bonds, real estate, and other assets to minimize risk while maximizing growth. Long-term investments, like stocks, generally yield higher returns and can help your money outpace inflation.

Budget Without Killing the Fun

Creating a budget doesn't mean giving up the things you enjoy. A good budget is about balance—it allows you to spend money on what matters most while keeping your financial goals in check. By planning ahead, sticking to a shopping list, and comparing prices, you can manage your money without feeling restricted. Budgeting isn't about deprivation; it's about making thoughtful choices so you can still indulge in activities and experiences that bring you joy, all while staying financially secure.

Kick High-Interest Debt to the Curb

Pay off high-interest debt as quickly as possible. Strategies like the debt snowball method, where you pay off your smallest debts first to build momentum before tackling larger balances, can help you stay motivated and organized. Avoid financing big purchases like new cars, and instead save up to pay in cash for a quality used car.

Build an Emergency Fund

Life happens, and an emergency fund is your safety net. Aim to save three to six months of living expenses. This cushion will keep you from derailing your financial goals when unexpected expenses arise.

Get Help When You Need It

A financial planner can offer tailored advice to help you hit your goals. Choose fee-only advisors to save money, as they charge a flat rate or hourly fee instead of taking a percentage of your investments. This approach avoids ongoing costs that can add up and reduce your overall returns over time.

Protect What You've Built

Wealth building isn't just about saving and investing—it's also about protecting your assets. Regularly review your insurance coverage, including health, car, home, and disability policies, and consider long-term care insurance to prepare for the unexpected. Monitor your spending, explore strategies to minimize taxes, and keep your financial documents well-organized.

Building wealth takes time, effort, and a clear strategy. By consistently making smart choices, you're on your way to achieving financial freedom. And remember, I'm here to help if you ever need guidance—visit my website anytime!

A QUICK TAKEAWAY:

You're rich when what you have is enough.

CHAPTER EIGHT

LIVING BIG BY DOWNSIZING

WELCOME TO THE JOY OF LESS

Downsizing. The word might make you think of sacrifices or cramped spaces, but it's actually about so much more than "having less." Downsizing is about simplifying your life, prioritizing what truly matters, and freeing yourself from the physical and mental clutter that can weigh you down.

Whether you're gearing up for retirement or just craving a fresh start, downsizing can be a liberating—and even fun—experience. Let's explore how to make this transformation smooth, exciting, and enjoyable.

WHY DOWNSIZE?

Downsizing offers numerous benefits that can simplify your life and improve your financial well-being. Living in a smaller home often means lower utility bills, reduced maintenance, and more time to focus on what truly matters.

Selling your current home can also free up the equity—the difference between your home's market value and what you owe on it—providing a financial cushion as you prepare for retirement.

Financial benefits are just one piece of the puzzle. Downsizing also opens the door to a simpler and more fulfilling lifestyle. Picture spending your weekends on hobbies or travel instead of cleaning a large house or tending to a sprawling yard. With fewer belongings to manage, you gain not just time, but also a sense of freedom and peace of mind.

Another bonus? There are fewer bathrooms to clean. No more scrubbing multiple showers or worrying about keeping unused rooms spotless. If you move somewhere with little or no yard, you can say goodbye to mowing the lawn or trimming hedges. That's time you can reclaim for what truly makes you happy.

Ultimately, downsizing is about creating a home that serves you—not the other way around. It's not about giving things up; it's about focusing on what brings you joy and designing a life that reflects your priorities.

Declutter Like a Pro

The first (and biggest) step in downsizing is decluttering. It can feel overwhelming, but you don't have to do it all at once. Think of it as a journey, not a sprint. Start with one room at a time, and ask yourself:

- **Do I need this?**
- **Does it bring me joy?**

If the answer is no, it's time to let it go.

Life in Action: Mary and John's Story

Meet Mary and John, a couple who decided it was time for a fresh start. After their kids left for college, they decided to downsize. Their four-bedroom house was packed with years of memories—and stuff. At first, the idea of going through everything felt daunting.

They started with the basement, uncovering old toys, forgotten holiday decorations, and broken gadgets. What could have been a stressful chore turned into a treasure hunt. They laughed over old photo albums, donated unneeded items, and made extra cash selling things online.

Of course, it wasn't all easy. Sorting through sentimental items like family heirlooms took time, and tough decisions brought emotional challenges. There were countless trips to donation centers, logistical hurdles with selling their home, and moments of doubt about whether it was all worth it.

When they finally moved into their cozy two-bedroom condo, the benefits became clear. With less cleaning, fewer repairs, and no yard work, they had more free time and less stress. Downsizing provided financial security, emotional freedom, and a fresh start.

Mary and John agreed it was worth it. They felt lighter, happier, and ready to embrace their next chapter. For them, downsizing wasn't just about moving to a smaller space—it was about gaining the freedom to focus on what truly mattered.

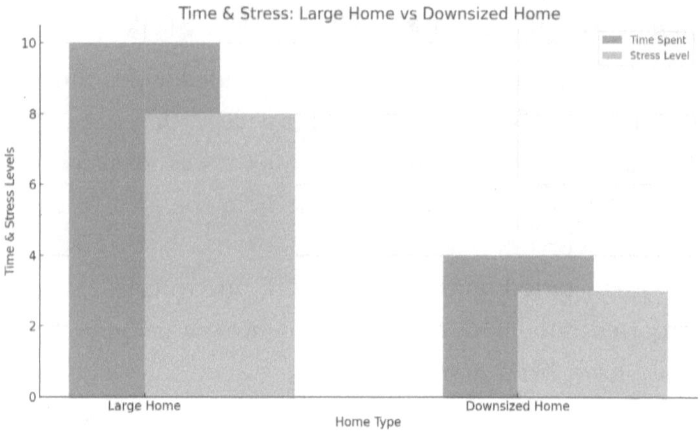

Understanding the Graph Above

This graph illustrates the difference in time and stress levels between maintaining a large home versus a downsized one. It highlights how larger homes often require more upkeep, leading to increased stress and less free time. Downsizing to a smaller, more manageable space can significantly reduce these burdens, allowing you to focus on what truly matters. It's a compelling reminder that sometimes, choosing less can actually give you more—more time, more freedom, and more peace of mind.

Need Help Getting Started?

If the thought of decluttering feels like an uphill battle, don't worry—you're not alone. Fortunately, there are plenty of resources and strategies to help make the process manageable and even enjoyable.

Marie Kondo's book, *The Life-Changing Magic of Tidying Up*, is a fantastic starting point. Her method encourages keeping only the items that "spark joy," making it easier to let go of things you no longer need. If you prefer a hands-on approach, consider hiring professional downsizing services. These specialists can guide you through the process, streamlining your belongings and reducing the overwhelm.

Prefer to take things slow? Start small. Choose one drawer, closet, or room to tackle at a time. Break the process into manageable chunks, like sorting through clothes one day and kitchen items the next. By setting realistic goals and working steadily, you'll make progress without feeling buried in the task.

Remember, you don't have to do this alone. Enlist help from family, friends, or professionals to share the workload and keep you motivated. Downsizing isn't just about decluttering—it's about creating space for a simpler, more fulfilling life. Take it one step at a time, and you'll get there.

Finding the Right Fit

Once you've decluttered, it's time to envision your next chapter. What does your ideal downsized home look like? For some, it's a cozy cottage by the lake, offering tranquility and charm. For others, it's a sleek condo in the heart of the city, with restaurants, theaters, and shops just steps away. Or perhaps you're drawn to the freedom of an RV lifestyle, hitting the open road and exploring new places at your own pace.

Life in Action: Tom's Story

Meet Tom, a lifelong dreamer of beachside living who always thought it was financially out of reach. After selling his suburban home and tapping into its equity, Tom moved into a 55-plus active living community near the coast. It wasn't the standalone beachfront condo he'd once imagined, but it checked all the boxes: close proximity to the ocean, a vibrant social scene, and amenities like a fitness center and pool.

Now, Tom begins his mornings with walks on the sand, soaking in the fresh sea air. His days are filled with activities he loves—joining clubs, meeting new friends, and participating in community events—all without the burden of home maintenance. By downsizing and prioritizing lifestyle over square footage, Tom found exactly what he was looking for. He couldn't be happier with his decision to embrace a simpler, more fulfilling way of living.

Downsizing isn't just about the size of your home—it's about choosing a lifestyle that aligns with your values and goals. Whether it's lakeside serenity, city excitement, or coastal relaxation, finding the right fit means prioritizing what truly matters to you.

Factors to Consider When Choosing a Downsized Home

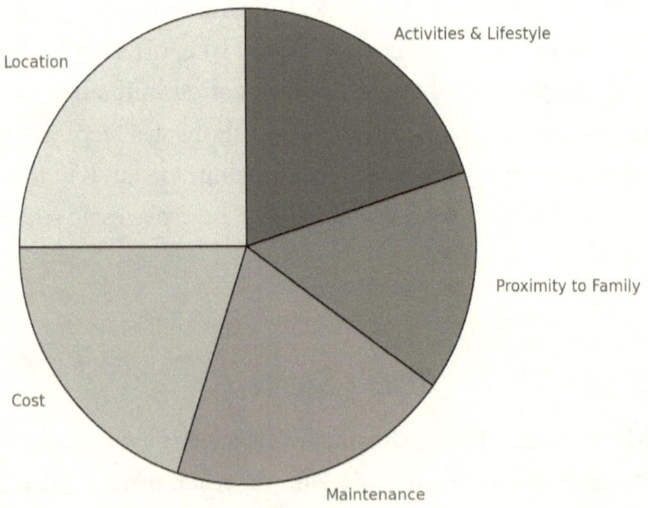

Understanding the Chart Above

This pie chart breaks down the key factors people commonly prioritize when choosing a downsized home: Location, Cost, Maintenance, Proximity to Family, and Activities & Lifestyle. Each segment highlights a different consideration, showing that selecting the right home is about finding a balance between these elements. Whether you value being closer to loved ones, reducing expenses, or enjoying a vibrant lifestyle, this chart serves as a reminder to weigh your priorities thoughtfully to create a downsized life that truly suits your needs.

Closing Thoughts

Downsizing isn't about losing—it's about gaining freedom and focusing on what's most important. By letting go of what no longer serves you, you create space for new opportunities, experiences, and a simpler, more intentional way of living. Whether your dream is to travel more, dive into new hobbies, or enjoy a low-maintenance lifestyle, downsizing can be the key to unlocking a lighter, more fulfilling chapter in life.

From a financial standpoint, downsizing often means reducing expenses, such as lower utility bills and maintenance costs, which allows more flexibility to spend on experiences, hobbies, travel, or anything else that brings you joy. So take that first step—sort through your belongings, pack up a box, and embrace the journey ahead. Downsizing may just be one of the most empowering and rewarding decisions you'll ever make.

A QUICK TAKEAWAY:

A balanced life comes from letting go of the excess and holding onto what's meaningful.

CHAPTER NINE

YOUR DREAM RETIREMENT BUCKET LIST

Big Dreams, Bold Moves

Retirement isn't just the end of your career—it's the beginning of an exciting new chapter with endless possibilities. For some, this might mean transitioning to part-time work, consulting, or pursuing a passion project instead of fully stepping away. However you picture it, retirement is your time to dream big, explore new interests, and finally turn those "someday" plans into reality.

Whether you've always wanted to travel the world, master a new skill, or give back to your community, now is the perfect time to start. Grab a pen and paper (or your favorite note-taking app) and let's begin crafting your ultimate retirement bucket list.

Why Create a Bucket List?

A bucket list isn't just a fun idea—it's a powerful way to focus on your most meaningful goals and aspirations. By writing down your dreams and priorities, you're more likely to make them happen. Plus, it gives you something exciting to look forward to—keeping you motivated every day.

Putting your goals on paper makes them real. When you write them down, you're not just dreaming—you're making a commitment to yourself. It turns vague ideas into clear intentions and gives you a roadmap to follow. A visual reminder of what you want helps keep you focused and accountable. It's not about wishing for a better life; it's about taking small, meaningful steps every day to make those dreams a reality.

Life in Action: Dave's Story

Dave spent years working long hours in a demanding job, always putting his own interests on hold. When he retired, he realized he finally had time to explore his passion for photography. He created a bucket list that included visiting national parks, documenting the beauty of nature through his camera, and taking an advanced photography course. Not only did this give him a renewed sense of purpose in retirement, but it also opened up a world of creativity and fulfillment.

For Dave, writing out his bucket list was a turning point. Once his goals were on paper, he felt more motivated to make them happen. Over the next few years, he visited several national parks, each trip reigniting his love for photography. He even entered a few local photography contests—something he never imagined doing. Looking back, Dave credits the simple act of writing down his dreams as the spark that inspired him to live a more intentional and fulfilling retirement. What started as a list of ideas turned into some of the best memories of his life.

Dave's story is a reminder of how powerful a bucket list can be in bringing purpose and excitement to your retirement. It's not just about writing down your dreams—it's about taking action to create the experiences that matter most to you. Now it's your turn. Create a bucket list that reflects your passions, dreams, and goals. Here's how to get started.

CRAFTING YOUR IDEAL RETIREMENT VISION

Step 1: Dream Without Limits

The first step in creating your retirement bucket list is to let your imagination run wild. Don't worry about the "how" just yet—focus on the "what." What have you always wanted to do, see, or experience? Whether it's skydiving, writing a book, or learning to play the guitar, no dream is too big or too small to make the list.

If you're feeling stuck, think back to your childhood dreams or the things you've always said you'd do "someday." Guess what? That "someday" has arrived, and it's time to make those dreams happen.

Here are some ideas to spark inspiration for your bucket list:

- **Learn a New Language:** choose a language you've always wanted to speak.
- **Visit All Seven Continents:** embark on a journey of travel and exploration.

- **Start a Business:** turn your passion into a fulfilling career or side venture.
- **Volunteer for a Cause:** give back to a community or cause that's close to your heart.
- **Go on a Road Trip Across Your Country:** discover the beauty and diversity of your homeland.
- **Complete a Triathlon:** challenge yourself with this ultimate multi-sport event.
- **Write and Publish a Novel:** share your story with the world.
- **Take a Photography Course:** learn to capture beautiful moments and stunning scenery.
- **Attend a Major Sports Event:** feel the excitement of experiencing it live.
- **Grow Your Own Food Garden:** embrace more sustainable and hands-on lifestyle.
- **Learn to Cook a New Cuisine:** master the flavor and techniques of a different culinary style.
- **Climb a Mountain:** conquer a peak that holds special meaning for you.
- **Create a Piece of Art:** paint, sculpt, or craft something uniquely yours.
- **Take a Meditation Retreat:** find peace and mindfulness in a calming new setting.
- **Visit a World Wonder:** witness one of the world's most awe-inspiring landmarks.

These ideas range from personal growth to adventurous experiences. Use them as a starting point, and choose the ones that resonate most with you. Craft a bucket list that reflects your dreams and creates a meaningful roadmap for this exciting chapter of your life!

Step 2: Prioritize Your Passions

Once you've created your list, it's time to prioritize. Which activities are "must-dos", and which ones are "nice-to-haves"? Consider practical factors like your budget, health, and timeline. Some dreams may be perfect for the early years of retirement when you're more active, while others might be better suited for later stages.

Step 3: Plan and Save for Your Dreams

Now that you have prioritized your list, it's time to start turning those dreams into reality. Some goals may be simple to accomplish, while others might take more time, effort and saving. Break each goal into smaller, manageable steps.

For example, if traveling is on your list, start by researching the best times to visit your chosen destinations, setting a realistic budget, and saving a little each month. Small, consistent actions can bring even your biggest dreams within reach.

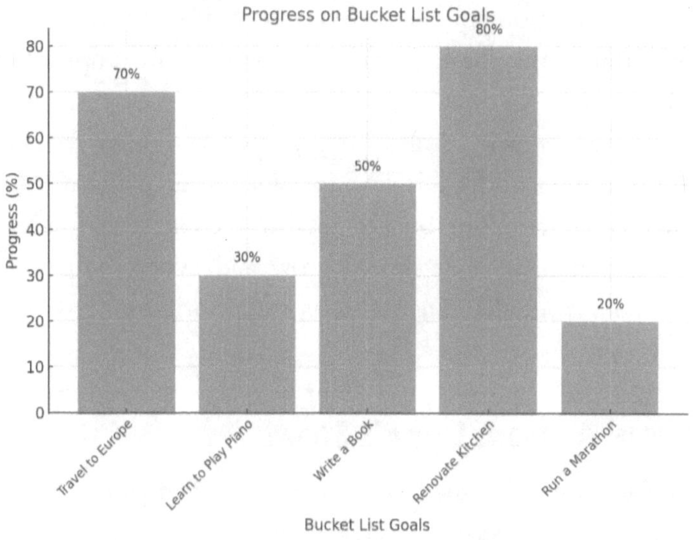

Understanding the Chart Above

This bar chart visually represents your progress toward achieving your bucket list goals. Each bar corresponds to a specific goal, with shaded sections showing how much you've completed so far. Tracking your progress this way makes it easy to see which goals are close to completion and which ones might need more attention..

Beyond simply monitoring your journey, this chart is a powerful motivator. It encourages you to keep moving forward and celebrates each achievement along the way. Seeing your progress laid out visually can inspire you to stay focused and enjoy the process of turning your dreams into reality.

Step 4: Enjoy the Journey

Having a bucket list is exciting, but the true value lies in the experiences you have along the way. While checking off items is satisfying, the journey itself is often where the most meaningful moments happen. Life is full of surprises, and sometimes the best memories come from unplanned adventures.

As you work toward your goals, stay open to new opportunities and be willing to adjust your plans if your interests shift. Your bucket list isn't set in stone—it's a living document that should grow and evolve with you, reflecting your changing passions and priorities.

Life in Action: Linda's Story

Linda always dreamed of exploring Italy, from strolling through the streets of Rome to sipping wine in Tuscany.

But as retirement approached, she also realized how important it was to spend time with her growing family, especially her grandkids. With two equally meaningful goals, Linda decided on a practical approach. She prioritized visiting Italy during the first few years of retirement, while she was still active enough to fully enjoy the physical demands of travel.

At the same time, Linda didn't want to miss out on everyday moments with her grandkids. To balance her bucket list, she made time for frequent, shorter visits with them. Now, she's even considering taking each grandchild individually to Italy and other travel destinations, starting with the oldest, to create unforgettable memories together.

By structuring her time around both big adventures and meaningful moments, Linda created a fulfilling plan. Her thoughtful prioritization allowed her to travel the world while cherishing time with her loved ones. Linda's story shows that with careful planning, you can pursue multiple dreams without sacrificing one for the other.

Life in Action: Mark's Story

Mark had always dreamed of hiking the Appalachian Trail solo, but he knew such a big goal required careful planning. Instead of feeling overwhelmed, he broke it down into manageable steps. He began by researching the trail, learning about the best seasons to hike, and making a list of the gear he'd need. On weekends he took smaller local hikes to build his endurance and ensure he was physically ready for the challenge.

Mark also realized the trip would require financial preparation, so he created a budget specific to his dream. He set aside a portion of his monthly savings for someone to take care of his home and pets, travel expenses, and time off work. Over several years, Mark gradually gathered everything he needed—physically and financially—to make his dream a reality.

By the time he retired, Mark was fully prepared. He had the experience, the equipment, and the savings necessary to embark on the adventure he'd been envisioning for years. His story is a testament to the power of patience, planning, and saving. Even the biggest dreams can be achieved, one step at a time.

Life in Action: Sue's Story

Sue had always dreamed of learning French and spending a year in Paris. When she retired, it became her top priority. She eagerly enrolled in French classes and immersed herself in French culture.

But something unexpected happened along the way—Sue discovered a passion for cooking. At first, she hesitated to shift her focus away from Paris, a dream she had cherished for years. However, as she dove into culinary classes, she realized that this new pursuit brought her just as much joy.

Although Sue never made it to Paris, she didn't feel unfulfilled. Instead, she found contentment and purpose in her newfound love for cooking—a path she hadn't anticipated but fully embraced. By letting go of her original dream and following this new direction, Sue learned that staying flexible with your bucket list allowed unexpected opportunities to flourish.

As you reflect on your own story, remember the importance of adaptability. If a goal no longer excites you or a new passion emerges, don't be afraid to change course. Life doesn't always unfold as planned, but pursuing what feels meaningful is what truly matters. Often, the most surprising paths lead to the greatest rewards, making your journey even more fulfilling. Stay open, and embrace the experiences that resonate with you.

Closing Thoughts

Creating a retirement bucket list isn't just about checking off boxes—it's about designing a life that reflects who you are and what brings you joy. It's an opportunity to revisit old passions, try new experiences, and focus on what truly matters. Think of retirement as a blank canvas, with your bucket list as the vibrant brushstrokes that bring it to life.

Remember, the journey is just as important as the destination. Some dreams might take time, and others may evolve, but that's all part of the adventure. Don't rush the process—savor each moment, celebrate your progress, and enjoy this exciting chapter of your life.

Whether your dream is to travel the world, learn something new, or spend more time with loved ones, now is the time to make it happen. So grab a pen, start your list, and take the first step toward living your dreams. You've worked hard for this—now make it unforgettable!

A QUICK TAKEAWAY:

Retirement is the time to chase the moments that make you smile and the dreams that make you feel alive.

CHAPTER TEN

LIFE AFTER WORK – FINDING YOUR GROOVE

EMBRACING THE FREEDOM OF RETIREMENT

Retirement is a lot like the first day of summer vacation as a kid—you're free. No alarms to set, no meetings to attend, and no work emails constantly pinging you. But once the initial excitement fades, you might find yourself asking, "Now what?" Let's explore what leaving the work force really means and how to navigate the emotional and psychological shifts it brings. Retirement isn't just about having more time; it's about redefining your purpose and embracing the freedom to live life on your terms.

FINDING YOUR NEW IDENTITY

For years, you may have introduced yourself with, "I'm [Your Name], and I'm a [Your Profession]." But now that work is no longer a defining part of your life, you might find yourself asking, "Who am I now?" This can be one of the most challenging questions to answer.

The key is to remember that you've always been more than your job title. This phase of life is an opportunity to rediscover who you are—or even reinvent yourself entirely.

Life in Action: Paul's Story

Paul had been fascinated with woodworking since he was young. He loved the idea of creating something with his own two hands—the smell of fresh-cut wood, the satisfaction of sanding a piece smooth, and the challenge of building something both beautiful and functional. But as life moved forward, woodworking became a passion he admired from a distance.

As a corporate lawyer, Paul's days were consumed by long hours, constant deadlines, and high stress. Between the demands of his job and the responsibilities of family life, he simply didn't have the time or energy to pursue woodworking in a meaningful way. His weekends were filled with catching up on work, attending events, and spending whatever moments he could with his family and friends. Woodworking became one of those "someday" dreams he'd revisit after retirement.

When Paul finally retired after 35 years, he felt unmoored. So much of his identity had been tied to his career that he wasn't sure who he was without it. Then, he remembered his old passion—woodworking. Without work obligations weighing him down, Paul decided it was time to take it seriously.

He cleared out a space in his basement, bought a few tools, and turned it into a workshop. He started small with simple projects like shelves but quickly built his skills—and his joy. Before long, he was crafting furniture, picture frames, and even custom pieces for friends. Woodworking gave Paul a new sense of purpose, something completely separate from his former corporate identity.

Now, when people ask Paul what he does, he proudly says, "I'm a woodworker." What started as a dream he had pushed aside for decades has become a core part of who he is. Unlike his high-powered legal career, woodworking brings him daily fulfillment and joy.

Paul's story shows how retirement can be the perfect time to rediscover an old passion or explore a new one. It's never too late to reinvent yourself or embrace something that makes you genuinely happy. For Paul, it took 35 years to get there—but now woodworking is what makes every day meaningful.

Who Are You Now?

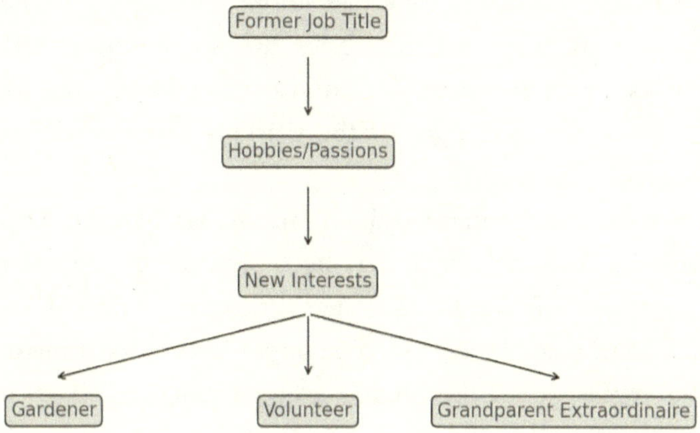

Understanding the Chart Above

This flowchart is designed to guide you in rediscovering your identity after a major life change, such as retirement or a career transition. It starts with your former job title and walks you through reflections on your hobbies, passions, and new interests. By the end, it suggests fun new identity options, like "gardener," "volunteer," or even "grandparent extraordinaire."

The process is valuable because it helps you embrace new roles and find joy in this next phase of life. By reflecting on what excites and fulfills you, the chart encourages you to move forward with confidence and a renewed sense of purpose.

Coping with the Loss of Work-Related Social Connections

Let's face it—work isn't just about the job. It's where friendships form, where stories are shared over coffee breaks, and yes, where you bond over venting about long hours or the challenges of the workplace (we've all been there!).

Retirement brings a sudden shift in that dynamic. Those daily interactions, which may have seemed routine, are no longer part of your life. For many, this can lead to feelings of isolation and loneliness. You might find yourself missing the camaraderie, the shared experiences, and even the comfort of seeing familiar faces every day.

Without that structure, the days can feel longer and lonelier, creating an emotional void. On top of that, there's the psychological adjustment. For decades, your work wasn't just a source of income—it was part of who you were. Whether you were the go-to person for advice, the office comedian, or the one who brought donuts every Friday, that role disappears when you leave the workforce.

The challenge now is finding new ways to fill those emotional and social gaps. It's completely normal to feel like you've lost part of yourself when you retire, but recognizing these feelings is the first step. From there, you can begin to reconnect with family, old friends, former colleagues, or neighbors, build new relationships through hobbies or community groups, and reinvent your social life for this new stage of life.

Life in Action: Susan's Story

Susan had been a teacher for 40 years, always surrounded by the buzz of a busy school day—students, colleagues, and the energy of a shared mission. When she retired, the quiet in her house felt overwhelming—"deafening," as she put it.

She missed the spontaneous hallway conversations, the collaborative lesson planning, and even the noisy lunch breaks with fellow teachers. For Susan, her work wasn't just a job; it was a source of daily interactions that gave her a sense of belonging and purpose.

At first, she struggled with the void. The silence felt isolating, and she found herself disconnected from the world she had known for so long. Her work had not only provided purpose but also a reason to leave the house and engage with others every day.

To bridge the gap, Susan reached out to a few former colleagues and started a weekly book club. What began as a small gathering quickly blossomed into a thriving social circle. She rekindled old friendships and met new people who shared her love of reading and conversation.

Susan realized that finding a balance between maintaining old connections and building new ones was key to easing the emotional challenges of retirement. Staying socially active helped her feel more grounded and less isolated.

Her story highlights the importance of replacing the social bonds lost after leaving work. Whether it's joining clubs, volunteering, or simply reconnecting with old friends, the most important thing is not to face retirement alone. Like Susan, you might discover that blending familiar connections with new experiences can make the transition smoother and more fulfilling.

Starting Your Next Adventure

Retirement isn't the end—it's the start of a brand-new chapter in your life. It's a time filled with opportunities you might never have imagined. The key is to welcome it with an open mind, even if it feels a little overwhelming at first.

Retirement opens up a world of possibilities. You finally have the freedom to pursue the things you've always dreamed of, without squeezing them into weekends or short vacations. This is your chance to explore new interests, dive into exciting hobbies, or simply slow down and savor the little moments that work often pushed aside.

Whether it's traveling the world, starting a passion project, spending more time with loved ones, or enjoying a peaceful morning walk, this phase is about discovering what truly brings you joy. See retirement as a fresh start—a chance to live life on your own terms.

Life in Action: Joyce's Story

Joyce spent 35 years as a civil engineer, managing large-scale projects, solving complex problems, and thriving in a high-pressure, male-dominated field. When she retired, she felt unmoored, unsure of how to fill her days. The structure and sense of purpose she had relied on for decades were suddenly gone, leaving an unsettling void.

Rather than dwelling on the uncertainty, Joyce made a bold decision—she booked a one-way ticket to New Zealand. Over six months, she explored breathtaking landscapes, hiked mountains, and immersed herself in Māori culture, even learning about their innovative infrastructure projects, which fascinated her as a former engineer. Along the way, she rekindled her love for photography, capturing stunning sunsets and wildlife that reignited her creative spark.

At first, the freedom felt overwhelming. Adjusting to life without the constant demands of her career was emotionally challenging. But as Joyce embraced the slower pace, she realized she wasn't just passing time—she was rediscovering who she was beyond her work. Meeting inspiring people, reconnecting with her passions, and finding moments of peace brought her a deeper sense of fulfillment than she had ever experienced during her busy work years.

Joyce's story is a testament to the transformative power of retirement. While it may come with emotional and psychological challenges, it's also a chance for reinvention and growth. It's not just about what you leave behind—it's about discovering all that you can gain when you embrace this new phase of life with an open mind and heart.

Retirement can be just as exciting and meaningful as your working years—perhaps even more so. It's all about how you choose to step into the unknown and make it your own.

Final Thoughts

Retirement is the start of a new adventure. While it comes with its challenges—particularly on the emotional and psychological side—it's also a time to rediscover yourself, reconnect with old friends (or make new ones), and finally tackle all the things you've been putting off for years. Take a deep breath, smile, and get ready to enjoy the journey.

Remember, you're not alone in this transition. Thousands of people are navigating it alongside you, and with a little humor, a touch of creativity, and an open mind, you'll find that retirement can be one of the most rewarding phases of your life.

So, what's your first step on this exciting new path? It's time to start exploring.

A Quick Takeaway:

The emotional and psychological challenges of retirement are real, but so are the opportunities to rediscover your passions and live life on your terms.

CHAPTER ELEVEN

RETIREMENT REIMAGINED - THRIVING IN AN UNPREDICTABLE WORLD

A New Era of Retirement

Retirement isn't what it used to be. The traditional path of working until 65, collecting a pension, and settling into a laid-back life with a gold watch—once a symbol of appreciation for decades of service—is a thing of the past. Today, retirement is about flexibility, achieving financial independence through your own savings and investments, and being prepared to adapt to life's unexpected challenges.

In this chapter, we'll explore how to redefine retirement in an ever-changing world. You'll learn strategies to secure your future, protect your financial stability, and confidently navigate whatever the economy might throw your way. And who needs a gold watch when you've got the freedom to spend your time however you choose? Retirement isn't just an endpoint—it's a dynamic phase full of opportunities, growth, and new beginnings.

THE POWER OF FINANCIAL INDEPENDENCE

Imagine retirement not because you've reached a specific age, but because you've achieved a level of financial freedom that lets you live life entirely on your terms. That's the true power of financial independence. It means having enough savings and investments to cover your living expenses without relying on a traditional job.

Financial independence opens doors to possibilities far beyond the conventional idea of retirement. You no longer have to wait until your 60s or 70s to enjoy the freedom that financial security provides. Instead, you gain the ability to choose how you spend your time—whether it's working part-time, pursuing passion projects, traveling the world, or dedicating yourself to causes that matter deeply to you.

This kind of freedom gives you control over your life, allowing you to escape the limitations of a 9-to-5 schedule and redefine what retirement means for you personally. Financial independence isn't just about money—it's about creating a life where you're in charge of your time and priorities.

It also provides peace of mind in an unpredictable world. During times of economic uncertainty, financial independence acts as a safety net. It enables you to adapt to changes—whether they're job-related, health-related, or unexpected shifts in the market—without worrying that your quality of life will be at risk. Achieving financial independence is more than a goal; it's a way to build security and flexibility for whatever the future holds.

LIFE IN ACTION: LISA'S STORY

Lisa is a great example of how financial independence can transform your life. In her thirties, she began saving aggressively, investing in low-cost index funds, cutting unnecessary expenses, and living below her means. Her disciplined approach paid off. By the time she turned 50, Lisa had achieved financial independence, freeing her from the traditional 9-to-5 grind.

Today, Lisa's life is anything but typical. She still works part-time, but only on projects that truly inspire her. Her financial freedom gives her the flexibility to travel whenever she wants, allowing her to explore new places and immerse herself in different cultures.

Lisa also dedicates her time to volunteering at her local animal shelter, supporting causes she's deeply passionate about. Her days are filled with purpose, balance, and the freedom to choose how she spends her time.

Lisa's version of "retirement" doesn't follow the conventional mold, and that's what makes it so rewarding. Financial independence gave her the power to design a life she loves—free from the constraints of a full-time job. Her story is a testament to how smart planning and discipline can create a future where you have the freedom to focus on what truly matters to you.

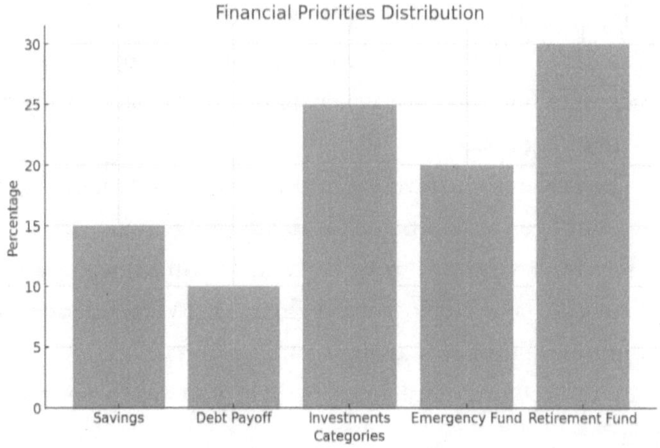

Understanding the Chart Above

This bar chart breaks down the distribution of financial priorities, showing key areas where you might allocate resources. These include savings, debt payoff, investments, building an emergency fund, and contributing to a retirement fund. Understanding how to balance these categories is an essential step toward achieving financial independence.

By visualizing your financial priorities, the chart helps you ensure that each area gets the attention it needs. This clarity allows you to make informed decisions, secure your financial future, and stay on track to reach your long-term goals.

STRATEGIES FOR REACHING FINANCIAL FREEDOM EARLY

Achieving financial independence isn't just for the wealthy or those with high salaries—it's possible for anyone with the right approach and mindset. The key lies in making consistent, intentional financial decisions that prioritize saving, investing, spending less, and living within your means. It's not always about earning more; it's about managing what you earn wisely and setting yourself up for long-term success.

The earlier you start, the more time your money has to grow, but even if you begin later, adopting smart strategies can fast-track your progress. By focusing on a few key areas, anyone can take steps toward financial independence, no matter where they're starting from.

Here are some strategies to help you reach your goal faster:

Save Aggressively

The more you save now, the sooner you'll reach financial independence. Aim to save at least 20-30% of your income—or more, if possible. The key is consistency. Make saving a non-negotiable priority, even if it requires cutting back on discretionary spending or adjusting your lifestyle. Over time, these savings will add up and bring you closer to your goal.

Invest Wisely

Your money should work as hard as you do. Investing in a diversified portfolio that matches your risk tolerance and timeline can significantly impact your financial future. Low-cost index funds are a popular choice because they offer broad market exposure with minimal fees, allowing your investments to grow steadily without being eroded by high costs. The power of compounding works best when you invest early and stick to your plan.

Live Below Your Means

It sounds simple, but it's crucial. The less you spend, the more you can save and invest. This means distinguishing between needs and wants, cutting unnecessary expenses, and focusing on what truly adds value to your life. Living below your means doesn't have to feel restrictive—it's about making deliberate choices that align with your long-term financial goals.

Build Multiple Income Streams

Don't rely on a single source of income. Explore options like side hustles, rental properties, or investments that generate passive income. The more income streams you have, the more secure your financial future becomes, and the faster you can achieve financial independence. Multiple income sources also provide a safety net in case one stream slows or stops altogether.

By incorporating these strategies into your life, you can accelerate your path to financial freedom and create a future full of flexibility and opportunity.

Life in Action: David and Elaine's Story

David and Elaine's experience shows how everyday people can achieve financial freedom through thoughtful planning and disciplined action. Both worked as teachers, earning modest incomes, but they had a clear vision for their future. Instead of spending their entire salaries, they chose to live frugally, directing a significant portion of their earnings into savings and investments.

Their major breakthrough came when they ventured into real estate. Over the years, they purchased several rental properties, which provided a steady stream of passive income. This additional income source allowed them to accelerate their wealth-building journey, even as they continued their teaching careers.

By their mid-fifties, David and Elaine had reached financial independence. The rental properties generated enough income to cover their living expenses, giving them the freedom to retire early. Also, they chose to continue working as part-time substitute teachers. This additional income stream not only provides extra financial flexibility but also allows them to stay active and connected to the profession they love.

Their story is a powerful reminder that you don't need a high salary to retire early. By making smart financial decisions, living below your means, and leveraging opportunities like passive income investments, you can create a life of financial independence. David and Elaine didn't achieve their dream by chasing wealth—they succeeded by being intentional with their money and taking control of their financial future.

Managing Investments in an Uncertain Economic Environment

The world is unpredictable, especially when it comes to the economy. We can't control economic downturns, inflation spikes, or market crashes, but with the right strategies, we can protect our financial independence and stay secure during rocky times. Financial independence isn't just about reaching a specific savings goal—it's about having a plan to maintain that security through life's inevitable ups and downs.

By preparing for uncertainty, you gain peace of mind and flexibility to weather whatever challenges come your way. With careful planning, you can ride out market fluctuations, adjust to inflation, and handle unexpected expenses without derailing your financial goals. The key is to stay proactive and adopt strategies that safeguard your financial foundation.

Here are a few strategies to help you stay secure:

Keep an Emergency Fund

Always have three to six months' worth of living expenses in a readily accessible account, like a savings or money market account. This cushion provides peace of mind and flexibility in case of unexpected expenses, medical emergencies, or income loss. An emergency fund acts as your financial buffer, allowing you to avoid dipping into long-term investments when life throws you a curveball. It's your first line of defense in uncertain times.

Diversify Your Investments

Don't put all your eggs in one basket. Spread your investments across different asset classes, such as stocks, bonds, real estate, and cash equivalents like money market accounts, certificates of deposit (CDs), or Treasury bills (T-bills). These low-risk, highly liquid assets help stabilize your portfolio during volatile periods. Diversification reduces risk by balancing your portfolio, so when one market struggles, another may thrive. This strategy helps you maintain balance and protect against significant losses.

Stay Informed, But Don't Panic

It's important to stay aware of economic changes, but avoid letting short-term market fluctuations influence your decisions. Panicking and selling investments during a downturn locks in losses, while staying calm and sticking to your long-term plan often yields better results. The stock market will have its ups and downs—it's natural. By keeping a level head, you can avoid rash, fear-driven decisions and stay on track with your financial goals.

Consider Inflation-Protected Investments

Rising living costs can slowly erode the value of your savings. To counter this, include assets that hedge against inflation, such as Treasury Inflation-Protected Securities (TIPS) or real estate. These investments adjust to rising prices, helping you maintain your purchasing power over time. Incorporating inflation-protected assets into your portfolio ensures that your money keeps working for you, even in an inflationary environment.

In Summary

By adopting these strategies, you can build a solid financial foundation that stands strong in uncertain times. Planning ahead empowers you to face economic challenges with confidence and keeps you on the path to financial independence.

Life in Action: Emily's Story

Emily, a retired nurse practitioner, is a great example of how preparation can help navigate unpredictable economic times. When a market downturn hit, her retirement savings took a significant dip. Many people in her position might have panicked, selling investments at a loss out of fear of losing even more. But Emily's careful planning and smart strategies made all the difference.

Because she had a diversified portfolio and a well-funded emergency account, Emily didn't have to touch her investments during the downturn. Instead, she relied on her emergency fund to cover her living expenses while waiting for the market to stabilize. Her patience paid off—over time, her portfolio recovered, and she avoided any permanent losses.

Emily's ability to stay calm and stick to her plan allowed her to protect her financial independence despite the economic uncertainty. Her story highlights the importance of being prepared with a diversified portfolio and a financial safety net. These strategies can help you weather the ups and downs of the market and maintain your financial security, no matter what challenges come your way.

Final Thoughts

Redefining retirement in an unpredictable world goes beyond just having enough money—it's about building a life where you have the freedom to spend your time exactly how you choose. Whether that's traveling the world, perfecting your golf swing, enjoying meaningful moments with loved ones, or even choosing to work part-time for added financial support and a renewed sense of purpose.

By prioritizing financial independence, creating diverse income streams, and managing your finances with care, you can craft a retirement that's not only secure but also adaptable to whatever life brings. The goal is a flexible, fulfilling future that reflects your unique vision and priorities.

Take charge of your financial journey today. Redefine retirement on your own terms, and make this phase of life one of the most rewarding chapters yet.

A QUICK TAKEAWAY:

We can't predict the future, but we can prepare for it. A strong financial foundation will weather any storm.

CHAPTER TWELVE

CRAFTING A ROUTINE THAT BRINGS YOU JOY

CREATING A MEANINGFUL AND FULFILLING DAILY ROUTINE

Life can sometimes feel like a series of tasks, where you wake up, go through the motions, and suddenly the day is over. Whether you're in the midst of your career or enjoying retirement, a daily routine that genuinely brings joy and purpose can transform how you experience each day.

In this chapter, we'll explore why building a thoughtful routine is so impactful, how to design one that fits your unique needs, and the benefits it can offer—no matter where you are in life. From boosting productivity to enhancing well-being, creating a routine you love can set the foundation for a more meaningful and satisfying life.

Creating a Rhythm for a Fulfilling Life

Routines aren't just about sticking to a schedule—they're about creating a rhythm that keeps your day grounded and purposeful. When your routine includes activities you enjoy and find meaningful, it adds structure and helps you wake up with a clear sense of direction. This applies whether you're at the start of your career, in the thick of it, or settling into retirement.

For those in their early or mid-career, a well-planned routine can help you manage your time, reduce stress, and ensure you're making space for the things that bring you joy. It's easy to get caught up in the hustle and forget to prioritize your own interests, but a thoughtful routine helps you balance work, personal passions, and self-care. It prevents life from feeling like it's rushing by without time for what matters most.

For retirees, a routine can be a game-changer. The sudden freedom after leaving the workforce is exciting but can also feel overwhelming. Work schedules and deadlines often provide a natural framework for daily life, and without them, the days can blur together. This lack of structure can lead to feelings of aimlessness or even depression. A routine anchors your days, bringing stability and giving you something to anticipate, whether it's a favorite hobby, social activity, or quiet time for yourself.

A fulfilling routine isn't about rigid schedules—it's about building balance, purpose, and joy into your daily life, whether you're climbing the career ladder or embracing retirement.

How to Build a Routine That Works for You

How do you create a routine that not only keeps your life organized but also brings joy and purpose? Here's a detailed look at steps you can take to build a routine that truly works:

Start with the Basics

Begin by identifying what you need to do every day. This includes essentials like eating meals, exercising, and daily responsibilities such as caring for family members, pets, or your home. These are the backbone of your routine—the non-negotiables that keep your life running smoothly. Spread these basics out in a way that doesn't overwhelm you, leaving room for activities you enjoy.

Identify Your Priorities

Beyond the basics, think about what truly matters to you. What are your long-term goals? What hobbies or activities make you feel most alive? Whether it's spending time with loved ones, volunteering, or pursuing a passion, these priorities should be an integral part of your daily or weekly routine. Determine how much time you want to dedicate to these priorities, ensuring they fit into your life without adding unnecessary stress.

Add in What Makes You Happy

Once the essentials and priorities are in place, focus on the activities that bring joy and fulfillment. Whether it's reading a great book, gardening, playing an instrument, or catching up with friends, make sure these things have a spot in your routine. These are the heart of your schedule, adding color and purpose to your days. Even small pleasures can have a big impact on your overall happiness.

Mix in Some Variety

Routines are helpful, but they can feel monotonous if they're too rigid. Keep things fresh by introducing variety. Try new hobbies, visit different places, or change up your exercise routine from time to time. Variety not only keeps your routine interesting but also challenges you to grow and step out of your comfort zone. Being a lifelong learner—whether it's through trying new recipes, learning a language, or exploring a new hobby—keeps your mind sharp and your days exciting.

Be Flexible

Life is unpredictable, and routines can sometimes get disrupted. That's perfectly fine! A good routine allows room for flexibility. Whether it's a last-minute invitation, an unexpected errand, or simply a day when you need to rest, adjust as needed and return to your routine when you can. Flexibility makes your routine feel natural rather than restrictive, enhancing your life instead of boxing you into a rigid schedule.

Reflect and Adjust

Periodically, take time to evaluate your routine. Is it still bringing you joy and helping you feel purposeful? If not, don't hesitate to make changes. Maybe you've discovered new interests you'd like to incorporate, or perhaps some activities no longer serve you as they once did. Regularly reassessing and tweaking your routine ensures it evolves with you and remains relevant to your life.

In Summary

By following these steps, you can create a routine that not only keeps your days organized but also reflects what truly matters to you. It's about striking the right balance between structure and spontaneity, ensuring your life is both grounded and filled with purpose, joy, and room to grow.

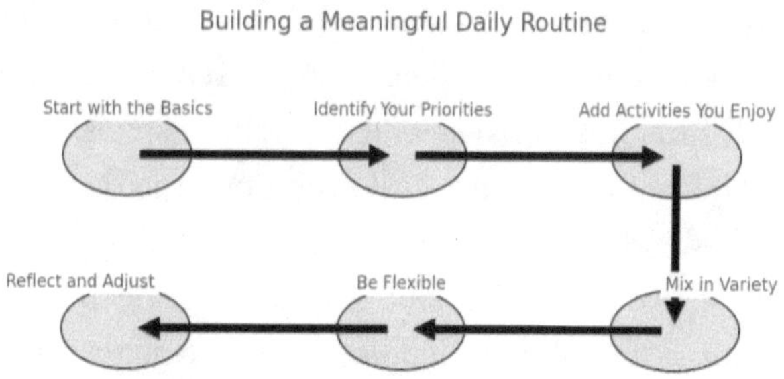

Understanding the Diagram Above

This diagram outlines the steps for creating a meaningful daily routine. It starts with the essentials—basic tasks and responsibilities—and gradually adds layers of personal priorities, enjoyable activities, and variety. The flow emphasizes the importance of flexibility and regular reflection to ensure your routine evolves with your changing needs.

By following this process, you can design a routine that brings structure to your day while also adding joy and purpose. This balance helps you stay grounded, fulfilled, and adaptable, no matter where you are in life.

The Benefits of a Joyful Routine

Creating a routine that brings joy and purpose to your life can have a profound impact on your overall well-being. It's not just about filling your schedule—it's about crafting a structure that makes you excited to face each day. A joyful routine balances the tasks you need to accomplish with the things you love to do, helping you find a rhythm that fits your lifestyle and personality.

When your routine reflects your values, interests, and goals, it becomes more than a series of activities—it's a pathway to a happier, healthier, and more fulfilling life. A routine you enjoy can give you a sense of control, accomplishment, and balance. It can reduce stress, improve mental and physical health, and even open the door to new friendships and learning experiences.

Life is unpredictable, but a good routine provides a foundation of stability, helping you manage whatever challenges come your way. It's not about rigid schedules—it's about creating moments of joy, connection, and purpose in your everyday activities.

Here are some of the key benefits:

Reduces Stress

A well-structured routine can make life feel less chaotic and more manageable. Knowing what to expect from your day provides a sense of predictability, which can be incredibly comforting in an unpredictable world. Setting aside time for relaxation, hobbies, and self-care helps reduce anxiety and stress, making your days feel more balanced.

Improves Mental Health

Activities that bring you joy have a positive impact on your mood and mental well-being. A well-balanced routine ensures you have time for both work and play, avoiding the mental fatigue that comes from neglecting self-care. Regular opportunities for reflection and growth help you maintain a positive mindset and emotional resilience.

Keeps You Active

A meaningful and fulfilling routine encourages both physical and mental activity, which are essential for health and vitality, especially in retirement. Regular exercise, whether it's a walk, yoga, or an active hobby, keeps your body strong. Similarly, mental activities like reading, puzzles, or learning new skills keep your mind sharp and engaged.

Provides a Sense of Accomplishment

Completing even small tasks can bring a sense of achievement when they're part of a routine. Checking items off your to-do list boosts motivation and self-worth, making you feel productive and satisfied with how you spend your time. These small wins reinforce positive habits and build momentum.

Enhances Your Social Life

Including social activities in your routine helps you stay connected with others, which is essential for emotional well-being. Whether it's a weekly coffee with a friend, joining a book club, or volunteering in your community, regular social interactions provide support, a sense of belonging, and opportunities for shared experiences.

Promotes Lifelong Learning

Incorporating learning into your routine keeps your mind sharp and opens up new possibilities. Whether you're taking a course, exploring a new hobby, or simply staying curious about the world, lifelong learning helps you stay adaptable, engaged, and excited about life.

In Summary

A joyful routine is more than just a schedule—it's a framework for living a life that feels balanced, meaningful, and fulfilling. By incorporating activities that align with your values, spark joy, and support your mental and physical health, your routine becomes a foundation for happiness and growth.

Whether it's reducing stress, staying active, or nurturing relationships, a well-crafted routine empowers you to approach each day with purpose and positivity. It's not about rigid schedules but about creating a rhythm that helps you navigate life's unpredictability while making room for what truly matters.

Crafting Routines That Balance Structure and Spontaneity

Retirement is your time to design a life that feels both organized and free. A thoughtful routine can help you stay productive, healthy, and engaged, while leaving room for the unexpected joys that make each day special. Here are a few examples of retirees who've struck the perfect balance:

Morning Focus: Helen's Energizing Start

Helen begins each morning with a structured routine to set a positive tone for her day. She starts with 15 minutes of stretching and a light walk around the neighborhood, followed by a cup of tea while journaling about her personal goals and heartfelt gratitude. By 10 a.m., Helen dives into a flexible part of her day, whether that's meeting friends for coffee, gardening, or exploring a local museum. Her mornings give her stability, while the afternoons leave space for spontaneity.

Creative Flow: Paul's Artistic Rhythm

Paul, a retired engineer, has built his retirement routine around his lifelong love of painting. He dedicates three mornings a week to working in his home art studio, experimenting with landscapes and abstract designs. Paul has even started attending a local art class to refine his skills and connect with other creatives. His afternoons are unstructured—some days he'll visit a new park with his grandkids, while others he'll relax with a novel from his favorite author or dive into a new story he's been curious about.

This blend of structured and open-ended time allows Paul to stay inspired and engaged without feeling confined to a strict schedule.

Adventure Days: Mark and Karen's Weekly Escape

Mark and Karen, a retired couple, maintain a flexible routine that still allows for excitement. Their weekdays are relatively predictable: exercise classes in the morning, errands or volunteering in the afternoons. But every Friday is their "adventure day." They might take a drive to a nearby town, hike a new trail, or try a restaurant they've never been to. These planned escapes add an element of surprise and keep their weeks feeling fresh.

Social Anchors: Joan's Community Connection

Joan organizes her week around a few social anchor points. On Mondays, she attends a local painting class. Wednesdays are reserved for volunteering at the library, and Fridays she participates in a book club. Between these commitments, her days are open for impromptu visits with family, long lunches with friends, or solo time to recharge. These anchor points give her life structure without feeling overbooked.

Open Saturdays: Tom's Free-for-All

Tom lives by the mantra "work hard, play hard—even in retirement." His weekdays are planned with productive mornings, such as managing his finances, maintaining his home, or pursuing hobbies like photography. Saturdays, however, are completely unstructured. He may wake up late, spontaneously decide to visit a farmer's market, or simply relax on the couch with a movie marathon. This contrast keeps him feeling refreshed and balanced.

Final Thoughts

Whether you're balancing a busy career or embracing the freedom of retirement, a well-crafted routine can be a game-changer. It's not about packing your days with tasks or following a rigid plan—it's about designing a rhythm that reflects your passions, values, and goals. A thoughtful routine helps you wake up each day with purpose and excitement, whether that means tackling creative projects, connecting with loved ones, or leaving space for spontaneous adventures.

As we've seen through the examples of retirees crafting routines that balance structure and flexibility, it's possible to create a schedule that works for you. Routines not only reduce stress but also keep you active, engaged, and connected—cornerstones of a happy and fulfilling life. Take inspiration from these stories and design a routine that gives your days meaning, joy, and a sense of balance.

This is your opportunity to make each day count, in ways that feel rewarding and true to you.

A Quick Takeaway:

The secret to a joyful life is found in the daily habits that bring meaning to each moment.

CHAPTER THIRTEEN

OVERCOMING RETIREMENT ROADBLOCKS

OVERCOMING THE BIGGEST CHALLENGES

Retirement planning isn't a one-size-fits-all process—it's a journey that evolves throughout your life. The hurdles you encounter in your twenties through your fifties, while you're building a foundation for the future, look very different from the challenges you'll face when you're actually retired. At every stage, there are unique obstacles to navigate, but they all have one thing in common: they require thoughtful planning and proactive decision-making.

The great news? Every challenge has a solution. Whether you're just starting your career, solidifying your financial footing, or enjoying your retirement years, there are strategies to address these pain points and move forward with confidence.

In this chapter, we'll break it down decade by decade. We'll explore the common challenges people face at each stage of life and discuss practical ways to overcome them so you can enjoy a secure and fulfilling retirement, no matter where you are on your journey.

Getting Started in Your Twenties with Limited Cash

The Pain Point

You're probably just starting out in your career, and retirement seems like a distant concern. But between student loans, rent, and just trying to get by, saving for retirement can feel impossible. Here's how to overcome retirement planning challenges in your twenties:

Start Small, But Start Now

Even with a limited budget, you can begin saving for retirement. Setting aside just $25 a month in a retirement account can grow significantly over time. The earlier you start, the more time your money has to compound, turning small contributions into substantial savings.

Prioritize Free Money

Take full advantage of your employer's 401(k) or 403(b) match, if offered. A 401(k) is typically available to employees in the private sector, while a 403(b) is common for those working in non-profits, schools, or government organizations. This match is essentially free money that boosts your retirement savings. Not contributing enough to get the full match is like leaving money on the table, so make it a priority if your budget allows.

Automate Your Savings

Set up automatic transfers to your retirement account to ensure consistent contributions. Automating the process removes the temptation to spend the money and helps you build a savings habit without extra effort.

In Summary

Starting your retirement journey in your twenties may feel like a stretch, but even small, consistent steps can create a strong foundation. By focusing on what's manageable now, you set yourself up for a more secure and flexible financial future.

Life in Action: Emma's Story

Emma, a 25-year-old marketing assistant, faced a familiar struggle for her generation—student loans, rent, and daily expenses left her living paycheck to paycheck. Saving for retirement felt impossible, especially with the added pressure of keeping up with social plans and everyday costs.

But a financial workshop offered to all employees during a company wellness week gave Emma a new perspective: she realized that even with her modest income, she could take meaningful steps toward planning and securing her financial future.

Instead of feeling overwhelmed, Emma decided to start small. She began contributing just 3% of her paycheck to her company's 401(k). At first, she doubted it would make much of a difference, and to her surprise, she hardly noticed the money was gone. Meanwhile, her retirement account started to grow. Encouraged, Emma set a simple goal to increase her contributions by 1% each year. The gradual increase allowed her to build her savings without making drastic lifestyle changes, and she appreciated that she could still enjoy her present while securing her future.

By age 30, Emma had built a solid nest egg, far ahead of many of her peers. Her employer's 401(k) match boosted her savings even more—a benefit she hadn't fully understood when she first started. She saw firsthand how starting early gave her money more time to grow and let compounding interest work its magic.

Emma's experience proves that starting small doesn't mean thinking small. By being consistent and taking manageable steps, she built momentum and created a strong financial foundation. Her story is a reminder that you don't need to make huge sacrifices in your twenties to secure your future. Small, steady contributions can lead to big rewards over time.

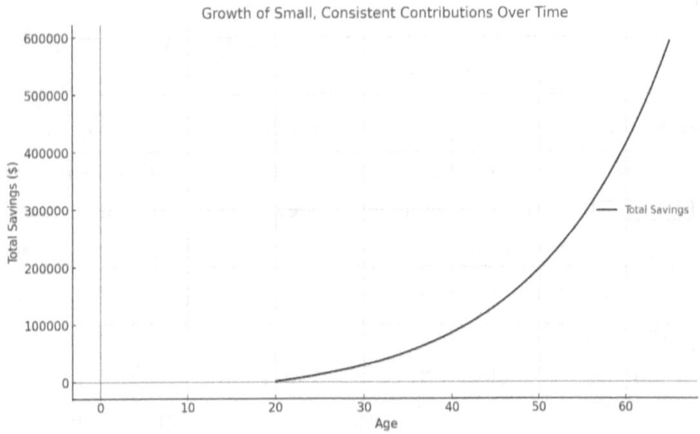

Understanding the Graph Above

This graph highlights the remarkable power of compound interest, showing how small, consistent contributions made in your twenties can grow into substantial savings by retirement. Starting early, even with modest amounts, gives your money more time to grow exponentially, like a snowball gaining momentum as it rolls downhill. By maximizing the time your savings can compound, you create a strong foundation for future financial security, proving that small steps today can lead to big rewards later.

Juggling Retirement, Career, and Family in Your Thirties

The Pain Point

By now, life is coming at you fast. You're raising kids, managing expenses, and focusing on advancing your career. With so many competing demands, it's easy to push retirement savings to the back burner. Here's how to overcome retirement planning challenges in your thirties:

Treat Retirement Savings Like an Expense

Automate your contributions so that saving becomes a consistent habit. By treating retirement savings as a non-negotiable expense—like your mortgage, rent, or utilities—you ensure it remains a top priority.

Watch Out for Lifestyle Inflation

As your income grows, the temptation to spend more on things like a bigger house, a fancier car, or lavish vacations can creep in. Instead, commit to increasing your retirement contributions each time you get a raise. It's a simple way to save more without feeling the pinch.

Take Full Advantage of Tax Benefits

Contribute to tax-deferred accounts like a 401(k) or IRA to reduce your taxable income while saving for the future. If your employer offers a 401(k) match, make it a priority to contribute enough to get the full match—it's essentially free money. Consider Roth accounts for tax-free withdrawals in retirement, giving you flexibility down the road.

In Summary

By prioritizing retirement savings as a non-negotiable expense, resisting lifestyle inflation, and maximizing tax-advantaged accounts like 401(k)s, IRAs, or Roth accounts, you can keep your financial future on track. These simple, intentional strategies allow you to juggle the demands of raising a family, managing expenses, and advancing your career while steadily building a secure foundation for retirement.

Life in Action: Mark and Lisa's Story

Mark and Lisa, both in their mid-thirties, were feeling the financial strain that so many families face—raising two young kids, paying expenses, saving for their children's education, and trying to move forward in their careers. Retirement? It felt like a far-off concern, something they could address "later." But after a serious conversation about their growing expenses and future goals, they realized that delaying retirement savings wasn't an option.

They didn't want to shortchange their kids or skip the occasional family vacation, but they knew they had to prioritize retirement savings without feeling overly stretched. That's when they developed a straightforward plan to make saving automatic and effortless.

Mark and Lisa set up automated contributions to their 401(k)s, treating these contributions like another monthly bill. This "set it and forget it" approach meant the money was invested before they had the chance to spend it elsewhere. It required no extra effort, but it kept their savings consistent.

They also made a pact: every time one of them got a raise or bonus, they would increase their retirement contributions by at least 1%. This strategy helped them avoid lifestyle inflation—a common trap where more income leads to more spending. Instead of splurging on the latest gadgets or upgrading their car, they used those raises to quietly grow their retirement funds.

At first, these changes felt small and barely noticeable. However, over time, their automated savings steadily grew. They continued to enjoy family vacations, cover their children's needs, and indulge in small luxuries, but now they had the added peace of mind that came with knowing their future was on solid ground. No longer living paycheck to paycheck, they were actively building a stable and secure financial future.

Mark and Lisa's story is a reminder that you don't have to choose between enjoying today and planning for tomorrow. With small, intentional steps—like automating savings and resisting lifestyle creep—you can balance your current needs with your future security. It's not about doing everything at once; it's about doing what you can, consistently, to ensure you're on the right track.

CATCHING UP ON MISSED SAVINGS IN YOUR FORTIES

The Pain Point

By your forties, retirement is no longer a distant concept—it's starting to feel real. If you didn't prioritize savings in your twenties or thirties, you might be feeling the pressure to catch up. The idea of closing the gap can feel overwhelming and even discouraging. Here's how to overcome the challenge of catching up on retirement savings in your forties:

Maximize Your Income

Your forties are often your peak earning years, making it a critical time to focus on increasing your income and building financial flexibility. This means having the resources to adapt to unexpected expenses, seize opportunities, or make decisions without being overly constrained by finances.

Whether it's advancing your career, developing new skills, or exploring additional income streams, the goal is to maximize your earning potential. Take advantage of opportunities your employer provides, such as earning bonuses or accessing professional development programs, and focus on activities that strengthen your financial position. By making the most of this decade, you can build greater stability and gain more control over your financial future.

Prepare for Catch-Up Contributions

Although catch-up contributions to tax-advantaged accounts like 401(k)s and IRAs don't begin until age 50, it's essential to start planning for them now. Your forties are often your peak earning years, making this an ideal time to increase your retirement savings and work toward the current contribution limits. By maximizing your savings now, you'll build a solid foundation that will allow you to take full advantage of additional catch-up contributions when you become eligible. The sooner you start, the more time your investments will have to grow, making it easier to close any savings gaps.

Reevaluate Your Investments

Take a close look at your portfolio to ensure it is diversified and aligned with your retirement goals. As you get closer to retirement, your risk tolerance and investment strategy might need adjustments. If you're unsure where to start, consider consulting a financial advisor to help optimize your plan.

In Summary

Catching up on retirement savings in your forties doesn't have to feel overwhelming. By boosting contributions, making smart use of extra income, and aligning your investments with your goals, you can make significant progress toward securing your financial future. It's not too late to take control and start building the retirement you envision.

Life in Action: Joe's Story

Joe was 42 when he had his financial wake-up call. Between raising kids, paying off a mortgage, and dealing with everyday expenses, retirement savings had taken a back seat. After looking at his accounts, he realized he was far behind where he needed to be. Determined to turn things around, Joe met with a financial advisor who helped him create a plan.

He started by increasing his retirement contributions, using automatic transfers to make savings a priority. Joe also rebalanced his investment portfolio to focus on higher-growth assets, knowing he still had time to ride out market fluctuations.

By age 50, Joe was ready to take full advantage of catch-up contributions. His disciplined approach to increasing savings and making strategic investments had steadily grown his retirement account, positioning him perfectly to use these additional contributions to accelerate his progress even further.

Joe's journey wasn't just about numbers—it gave him peace of mind and a renewed sense of control over his financial future. His story shows that even if you're behind, taking proactive steps now can set you back on the right path. With the right strategy and commitment, catching up is not only possible but achievable.

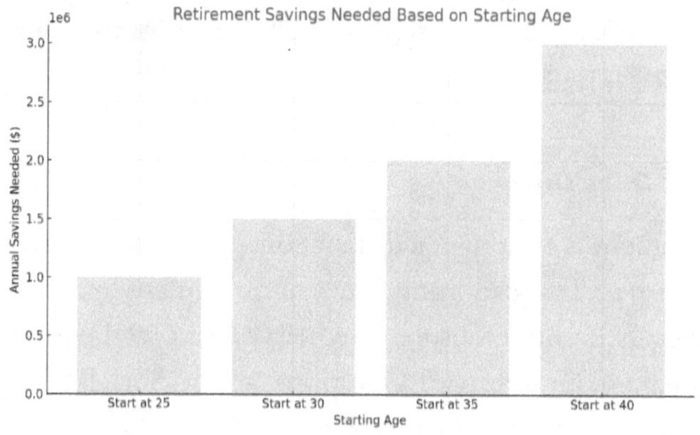

Understanding the Chart Above

This bar chart emphasizes a crucial point: the earlier you start saving for retirement, the easier it is to reach your financial goals. The chart shows the annual savings needed (in thousands of dollars) to accumulate $1 million by retirement age, depending on when you begin saving. For example, saving $500 annually is shown as 0.5, while $2,000 annually is shown as 2.0.

Starting at 25 allows you to save smaller amounts each year because compounding has more time to grow your investments. However, waiting until 40 significantly increases the annual savings required, as there's less time for your money to work for you.

The takeaway is clear—the later you start, the harder your money has to work, and the more you'll need to save annually. This chart highlights the value of starting early, even with modest contributions, to reduce the financial burden and create a smoother path to retirement security.

PREPARING FOR THE REALITY OF RETIREMENT IN YOUR FIFTIES

The Pain Point

Retirement is no longer a distant concept—it's right around the corner. This can bring a mix of excitement and anxiety, especially if you're unsure whether you've saved enough to maintain your lifestyle. Questions about Social Security, healthcare, and whether your nest egg is sufficient start to weigh heavily. Here's How to Overcome This Challenge:

Calculate Your Retirement Number

Take time to determine how much you'll actually need to retire comfortably. Consider expenses like healthcare, housing, travel, and the lifestyle you envision. Knowing your number gives you a clear target and helps you plan accordingly.

Shift to Conservative Investments

As you get closer to retirement, protect your hard-earned savings by transitioning to more conservative investments. This strategy helps reduce the impact of market downturns, ensuring that your nest egg remains stable when you need it most.

Consider Delaying Social Security

If you're able, delaying Social Security until age 70 can significantly boost your monthly benefits. This extra income can provide a more reliable financial foundation throughout your retirement years.

In Summary

In your fifties, the focus shifts to finalizing your plans and reducing financial risks. By knowing your retirement needs, protecting your savings, and optimizing your Social Security strategy, you'll be better prepared for a secure and enjoyable retirement.

LIFE IN ACTION: SANDRA AND ALEX'S STORY

At 55, Sandra had always been a diligent saver. But as retirement loomed closer, doubts started creeping in. She had worked hard, raised two kids, and now, with retirement on the horizon, she wasn't sure if she had done enough to secure her financial future. News headlines about fluctuating markets and rising healthcare costs didn't help. Sandra often found herself lying awake at night, wondering if she'd have to compromise her dreams of traveling or enjoying the small luxuries she'd worked so hard for.

Sandra wasn't facing this uncertainty alone. Her partner, Alex, had been a steady and supportive presence in her life, and the two often discussed their shared vision for retirement. Initially, Sandra hoped to retire fully at 62, but after meeting with a financial planner, she realized that transitioning to part-time work for three years and retiring fully at 65 would significantly improve their financial stability.

With this plan, Sandra shifted some of her investments to more conservative options, reducing exposure to market volatility and protecting her savings. The planner also recommended delaying Social Security until age 65, which would provide Sandra and Alex with a more comfortable income to support their retirement lifestyle.

Alex adjusted her plans as well, and together they agreed to prioritize part-time work and additional savings during this transitional period. These few extra years of earning and saving gave them the confidence to embrace retirement without financial worry.

Now, Sandra and Alex are focused not just on retiring but on creating a retirement filled with the adventures they've dreamed of together. They look forward to traveling, spending time with family, and enjoying their retirement years with confidence and joy. Sandra's story shows that thoughtful planning and a willingness to adapt can transform retirement into a secure and fulfilling chapter of life.

Managing Money and Maintaining Purpose in Retirement

Congratulations—you've made it to retirement! But reaching this milestone comes with a new set of challenges. It's not just about having saved enough; it's about making your money last and finding a sense of purpose now that the daily structure of work is gone.

The Pain Point

The fear of outliving your savings is a common and valid concern. With people living longer than ever, retirement could span 20, 30, or even 40 years. The challenge is ensuring your savings can support you throughout this time without running dry.

Retirement isn't just about financial management—it's also about redefining your sense of purpose. Without the routine of a career, it's easy to feel adrift. This stage of life requires balancing careful money management with meaningful activities that keep you engaged and fulfilled. Here's how to overcome the challenge of managing money and maintaining purpose in retirement:

Diversify Your Income

Don't rely solely on Social Security to fund your retirement. Look into additional income streams, such as part-time work, rental properties, or dividend-paying investments. These can provide extra financial stability and help stretch your savings over the long haul.

Adjust Your Spending

Keep a close eye on your spending by tracking where your money goes each month. If your budget feels tight, focus on covering essential expenses like housing, healthcare, and groceries. Then look for areas where you can cut back on non-essentials without sacrificing what brings you joy.

Consider a Guaranteed Income

Products like annuities can offer a dependable income stream for life, helping you cover your basic needs without worry. These financial tools are especially helpful for reducing the stress of unpredictable markets or fluctuating investment returns.

In Summary

By diversifying your income, staying mindful of your spending, and exploring guaranteed income options, you can approach retirement with confidence. This balanced approach allows you to focus on enjoying your retirement years without the constant fear of running out of money.

Healthcare Costs in Retirement

The Pain Point

As you age, healthcare costs will increase. It's one of the biggest financial concerns for retirees. Here's how to overcome the challenge of managing healthcare costs in retirement:

Maximize Medicare

Take time to fully understand your Medicare options, including Parts A, B, C, and D. Research supplemental insurance plans, such as Medigap or Medicare Advantage, to help cover out-of-pocket costs that Medicare doesn't. This extra coverage can save you from unexpected medical bills and provide peace of mind.

Plan for Long-Term Care

Long-term care insurance can be a lifesaver if you need extended care, whether at home, in an assisted living facility, or a nursing home. Start researching policies early to lock in lower premiums and ensure you're prepared for future healthcare needs.

Stay Healthy

Preventative care is one of the best ways to manage healthcare costs over time. Schedule regular check-ups, stay active with regular exercise, and prioritize a balanced diet. Taking care of your health now reduces the likelihood of costly medical issues down the road.

In Summary

By proactively managing your Medicare options, planning for long-term care, and focusing on a healthy lifestyle, you can significantly reduce your healthcare expenses in retirement and feel more secure about your future.

Loss of Purpose and Social Connections in Retirement

The Pain Point

After years of working, it's normal to feel a sense of loss when you no longer have a structured routine or professional identity. Without the daily purpose and social interactions that work provides, it's easy to feel adrift or isolated. Here's how to overcome the challenge of finding purpose and connection in retirement:

Build a New Routine

Just because you're not working doesn't mean you can't have a daily schedule. Structure your days with activities that bring joy and fulfillment, such as hobbies, exercise, or regular social engagements. A routine gives your days rhythm and ensures you have something to look forward to.

Stay Engaged

Use this time to explore new hobbies, revisit old passions, or give back through volunteer work. Keeping your mind active and your heart fulfilled can make retirement a period of growth, discovery, and satisfaction.

Stay Social

Maintain strong social connections by engaging with friends, family, or community groups. Join clubs, attend local events, or simply schedule regular meet-ups with loved ones. Staying connected is essential for emotional well-being and combating feelings of isolation.

In Summary

By creating a meaningful routine, pursuing fulfilling activities, and nurturing social connections, you can build a retirement that feels purposeful and vibrant. This stage of life is an opportunity to redefine your identity and focus on the things that truly matter to you.

Life in Action: David's Story

David had spent his entire career as a high school teacher, and when he retired at 65, he felt a mix of excitement and uncertainty. He had worked hard, saved diligently, and looked forward to the freedom that retirement promised. But once the dust settled, the reality of managing his money and maintaining a sense of purpose without the daily structure of work set in. With a retirement that could stretch 20 years or more, David knew he needed to make his savings last while also finding meaning in this new phase of life.

David's first concern was financial security. The idea of outliving his savings was a nagging fear. To tackle this, he diversified his income. In addition to Social Security benefits, David turned his passion for teaching into part-time tutoring. He also rented out a small guesthouse on his property, providing him with a steady stream of extra income. These additional revenue sources reduced the pressure on his savings and gave him peace of mind, knowing he had multiple safety nets.

Tracking his spending became a key part of David's financial strategy. While he still enjoyed traveling and dining out, he made sure to prioritize essentials like healthcare, housing, and utilities. When his budget felt tight, he made small, manageable changes—like canceling unused subscriptions and opting for budget-friendly vacations closer to home. These adjustments allowed him to maintain his quality of life without unnecessary financial stress.

Healthcare was another priority. Understanding the potential for rising medical costs, David took the time to research Medicare and opted for a supplemental insurance plan to cover any gaps. He also focused on preventive health measures, incorporating regular exercise and a healthy diet into his routine. These efforts not only reduced his medical expenses but also improved his overall well-being.

Beyond finances, David faced the challenge of filling his days with purpose. After decades of teaching, the loss of routine left him feeling restless. To rebuild structure, he created a new daily routine that included tutoring, volunteer teaching at a local community center, and dedicating time to hobbies like woodworking and gardening. These activities gave him a sense of accomplishment and fulfillment, helping him transition into this new chapter with confidence.

David also recognized the importance of staying socially connected. No longer surrounded by coworkers and students, he joined a local gardening club and organized a weekly coffee meet-up with retired friends. These social interactions kept him engaged and emotionally grounded, adding joy and connection to his days.

David's story shows that retirement isn't just about financial planning—it's about creating a balanced life that addresses money, health, and purpose. By diversifying his income, managing his expenses wisely, staying proactive about his health, and building a meaningful routine, David turned his retirement into a fulfilling and secure chapter. His approach serves as a reminder that with the right strategies, retirement can be just as rewarding as your working years.

Final Thoughts

Retirement planning isn't a one-size-fits-all process. The challenges you face in your twenties differ greatly from those in your fifties or the adjustments you'll make once you're retired. No matter where you are in your journey, the key is to take proactive steps that address your unique circumstances and move you closer to your goals.

It's not just about reaching retirement—it's about thriving in it. By confronting the hurdles of each stage head-on, from saving early to managing purpose and finances in retirement, you can build a future that's both financially secure and deeply fulfilling. The choices you make today will shape the retirement you enjoy tomorrow, so take charge and embrace the opportunities ahead.

Retirement is a chapter you get to write, so make it one filled with peace of mind, purpose, and joy.

A QUICK TAKEAWAY:

Success in retirement is not about escaping work; it's about embracing a life of purpose and balance.

CHAPTER FOURTEEN

LIFE PLANNING 101 - DESIGNING YOUR DREAM LIFE

START WITH YOUR DREAMS, NOT THE NUMBERS

Have you ever taken a moment, maybe with a cup of coffee (or tea if that's more your style), and imagined what your life could look like if money wasn't a constant worry? It's a big thought, isn't it?

Most of us approach budgeting, debt repayment, and saving for retirement by diving straight into numbers, spreadsheets, and financial goals. But what if we flipped the script? What if, instead of starting with the math, we started with a clear vision of what we truly want out of life? That's where *life planning* comes in—it's about identifying your dreams first and then aligning your financial decisions to make them a reality.

Life planning shifts the focus from numbers to what really matters: your aspirations, values, and sense of purpose. This approach helps you design not just a financial plan but a life that reflects your dreams. Let's dive deeper into how life planning can transform the way you think about your future.

What is Life Planning?

Life planning takes a refreshing approach to finances by focusing on what truly matters to you—your dreams, values, and the life you envision—before getting into the financial details. It's about crafting a plan that prioritizes joy, purpose, and alignment with your deepest aspirations, making your financial choices a means to achieve the life you desire.

George Kinder, often referred to as the father of life planning, emphasizes looking beyond the traditional retirement goals. His philosophy centers on identifying what's most important to you and building a financial strategy around that vision. It's not just about managing money; it's about creating a life that feels meaningful and intentional every step of the way.

The Three Questions to Change Your Life

George Kinder introduced three powerful questions to help you figure out what matters most. These aren't your typical "Where do you see yourself in five years?" type of questions. They dig deeper, challenging you to get honest about what you truly want.

Feel free to answer them in any order that feels right to you—there's no wrong way to reflect on your dreams. So grab a pen and jot down your thoughts as you read them:

1. **If you had all the money in the world, how would you live your life?**

   Picture this: you wake up tomorrow, and poof, financial worries are gone. How would you spend your days? Would you travel, learn new hobbies, spend more time with family? This question is about dreaming big without limitations.

2. **If you only had 5 to 10 years left to live, what would you do differently?**

   Reality check—time is limited. If you knew you only had a handful of years left, how would you change your life? Maybe you'd work less and play more. Perhaps you'd finally take that pottery class or spend more time with loved ones.

3. **If you had 24 hours left, what would you most regret?**

   This question is deep. If you knew you had just one day left, what would haunt you? Would it be the places you didn't go, the dreams you didn't chase, or the people you didn't spend enough time with? This question helps you laser-focus on what really matters.

These three questions are more than just thought exercises; they serve as a roadmap to uncover what brings you true joy and purpose. By answering them at your own pace and in your own way, you can start shaping your life around what truly matters. This process helps you prioritize your goals and live with greater intention. With a clearer picture of your ideal life, let's explore why life planning is so important and how it can guide you toward making those dreams a reality.

Why Is Life Planning Important?

Life planning goes beyond dreaming—it's about turning those dreams into a blueprint for your financial goals. After all, what's the point of money if it's not helping you live the life you truly want?

Think of life planning as setting the GPS for your finances. Before you can figure out the best route, you need to know your destination. Once you have a clear vision of where you're headed, the steps like budgeting, saving, and investing start to fall into place. These aren't just tasks; they're tools guiding you toward your dream life—not just a balance in your bank account.

Life in Action: The Travel Bug Dream

Imagine you've always had a passion for traveling. Exploring new places, immersing yourself in different cultures, and tasting cuisines from around the globe bring you joy like nothing else. You've spent years dreaming about retirement as a time to wander through cobblestone streets in Europe, savor fresh pasta in Italy, sip wine in a quaint French village, and lose yourself in art and history. This isn't just a fleeting thought—it's a vision that truly excites you.

Traditional retirement advice might say, "Save X dollars for a comfortable retirement." But what does that even mean? Comfort is vague; it's not personal or inspiring.

Enter life planning, which takes your dream and turns it into a focused, actionable goal.

Instead of thinking, "I need to save for retirement," life planning shifts your mindset to, "I want to spend three months each year traveling through Europe." That change is transformative. Suddenly, saving for retirement isn't about an abstract future—it's about fueling your passion.

With this specific goal in mind, your financial plan becomes personalized. You begin asking practical questions: What will flights cost? Where will you stay? How much will you need for food, museum tickets, and yes, as much gelato as you can eat?

Breaking your dream into these tangible steps gives your savings a clear purpose. Each dollar you save isn't just for "someday"; it's for that gondola ride in Venice, that Parisian café, or that art tour in Florence.

The beauty of life planning lies in aligning your finances with your passions. Each decision—whether it's downsizing your home, prioritizing travel over material purchases, or picking up a side hustle—becomes an investment in the life you want to live.

Saving for a dream like this doesn't feel like a sacrifice; it feels like anticipation. Every time you set money aside, you're getting closer to those adventures you've envisioned.

The takeaway? When you focus on what truly lights you up, life planning turns financial goals into something deeply motivating. It transforms vague plans into vivid dreams, helping you build a future filled with meaning and joy.

So, if travel is your dream, imagine it in full detail. Picture the laughter, the sights, the flavors, and use that vision to shape your financial choices. With life planning, you're not just saving for retirement—you're creating a life that excites you.

How to Accomplish Your Life Plan

Creating a life plan is about turning your dreams into actionable steps that guide your decisions. It's not just about imagining what you want—it's about setting clear goals and aligning your finances to make those dreams a reality. Here's how you can start building a life plan that works for you:

Clarify Your Vision

Start by diving into Kinder's three questions and answer them with complete honesty. Don't hold back—let your imagination run wild. What would make your life truly fulfilling? Dream big and think about the things that bring you joy, purpose, and excitement.

Set Meaningful Goals

Once you've clarified your vision, turn those dreams into actionable, tangible goals. For example, if you've always envisioned starting a small business in retirement, outline the details. What kind of business will it be? How many hours a week will you dedicate to it?

If giving back to your community is your passion, define what that looks like. Will you volunteer at a local organization, mentor young people, or even start a nonprofit? The more specific your goals are, the more achievable they become.

Make a Financial Plan

Now that you know what you want, it's time to make it happen financially. Create a budget that aligns with your goals. For instance, if your dream is to travel, start setting aside a dedicated travel fund. Break it down into categories like flights, accommodations, meals, and activities. Every goal comes with costs, so tailor your financial plan to reflect your priorities.

Review and Adjust

Life doesn't always go as planned, and your dreams may shift over time—and that's completely normal! Regularly review your life plan and make updates as needed. Perhaps you've discovered a new passion, like learning to play the cello, writing a novel, or diving into astrophotography, or your priorities have changed due to life circumstances. A flexible and evolving plan ensures your goals stay aligned with your current vision for the future.

In Summary

Your life plan is a dynamic tool to guide you toward the life you've always wanted. By clarifying your vision, setting meaningful goals, creating a budget, and staying open to adjustments, you can stay on track while allowing room for growth and new opportunities. This process ensures that your financial resources are working to support your dreams, helping you live a life full of purpose, joy, and fulfillment.

Adding Humor to Life Planning

Life planning doesn't have to be all serious faces and spreadsheets. It's okay to laugh at the fact that your dream of becoming a world-class ballroom dancer in your seventies might not be *entirely* realistic—but who cares? The beauty of life planning is in the dreaming. It's meant to be an exciting and optimistic process, not something that adds stress. After all, financial planning becomes way more fun when it's tied to ideas that make you smile.

Let's say your ballroom dancing dream doesn't involve a sparkling trophy. What about taking weekly dance lessons with friends or going on a dance-themed cruise? These smaller, more achievable dreams still bring joy and are absolutely worth planning for. The point isn't whether the dream is "big enough" or "practical"—it's about using your finances to support the things that light you up, especially if they come with a bit of humor along the way.

The magic of life planning is that it's personal. It's about figuring out what makes you happy and designing a life that reflects those joys. And yes, the journey might involve shifting goals or realizing some dreams are better as daydreams, but that's part of the fun! You're creating a plan that's flexible, meaningful, and uniquely yours.

When your life planning goals make you laugh or smile, they become easier to stick with. A vision that's full of personality and heart is far more motivating than a generic plan for "financial security." So, dream big—or small, or weird. Lean into what makes you happy and let your finances support that vision.

The key? Stay true to yourself. Adjust as needed, keep it lighthearted, and remember that the purpose of life planning is to help you enjoy the journey as much as the destination.

How Much of Your Budget Fuels Your Dreams?

It's easy to get caught up in the day-to-day grind of paying bills and managing expenses. But have you ever stopped to ask yourself: "How much of my budget actually supports the life I truly want to live?"

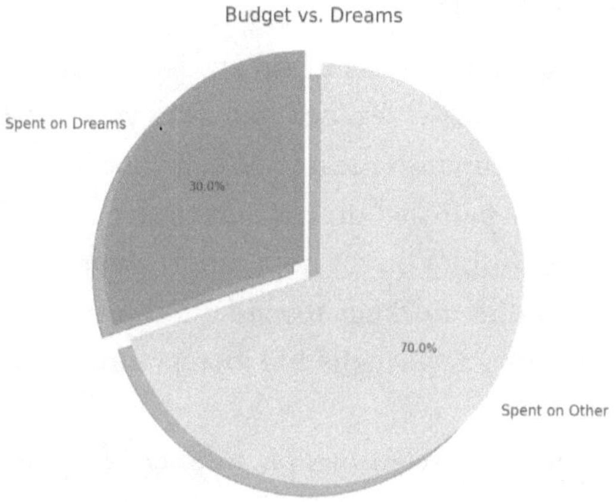

Understanding the Chart Above

The pie chart illustrates how your current budget breaks down—highlighting the portion spent on things that fuel your dreams versus areas that may not align with what you care about most. For many, this visual can be a wake-up call. You might discover that a surprising amount of money goes toward things that don't bring you closer to the life you envision.

This insight is powerful. Recognizing where your money is going can inspire you to realign your spending. If a large slice of your budget is devoted to things that don't bring joy or purpose, it's worth reevaluating how you allocate your funds.

By shifting more of your spending toward what truly matters—whether that's travel, hobbies, or other personal goals—you ensure your financial plan works for *you*. It's not just about covering the basics or maintaining the status quo; it's about building a life that reflects your dreams and values.

Closing Thoughts

Life planning isn't just about saving for a rainy day—it's about crafting a life that excites you, gives you purpose, and sprinkles a little fun into the mix. When your financial goals are tied to your personal dreams, every step you take feels more meaningful. You're not simply working toward retirement; you're working toward the life you've always envisioned, with a few laughs and joyful moments along the way.

So go ahead—dream big, plan thoughtfully, and don't forget to have fun with it. Whether your dreams are grand or modest, the most important thing is to begin. Let your vision guide your financial choices, and watch as those choices bring your ideal life closer with every passing day.

Remember: no dream is too bold, no goal is too quirky, and no financial step is too small. The journey starts now—one thoughtful, purposeful, and joy-filled step at a time.

A Quick Takeaway:

A dream without a plan is just a wish; life planning turns those wishes into reality.

CHAPTER FIFTEEN

THE ULTIMATE DECADE-BY-DECADE BUDGET GUIDE

Master Your Money, One Decade at a Time

Planning for retirement begins with the financial decisions you make in your twenties and grows as your life evolves. Every choice—whether it's saving from your first paycheck or managing withdrawals in retirement—shapes your financial future. The earlier you begin, the more secure your future can be. And here's more good news: creating and sticking to a budget isn't as daunting as it sounds.

I saved this chapter for last because, let's face it, the word *budget* can make some people cringe. It might even bring back memories of high school math class. But don't worry—this isn't about complex equations or endless spreadsheets. Think of this chapter as a friendly guide, not a tedious chore.

We'll walk through everything you need to create a budget that evolves with you. Whether you're starting out in your career, navigating the expenses of family life, or preparing for retirement, this chapter has you covered. You'll learn how to use tools like spreadsheets or budgeting apps to track your income, set meaningful goals, and adjust your budget as your priorities shift.

This isn't just about numbers; it's about empowering you to take control of your financial life. A well-maintained budget gives you the confidence and clarity to make the most of your hard-earned wealth. It's a tool to help you achieve your dreams, minimize stress, and enjoy greater peace of mind.

By the end of this chapter, you'll understand how to create and maintain a budget that works for your unique circumstances—one that's easy to update as life changes. With the right approach, you'll be prepared to tackle financial challenges and stay on track for a smooth, secure, and fulfilling retirement.

Your Twenties: Laying the Foundation

Your twenties are the perfect time to develop smart financial habits that will set the stage for long-term success. As you start managing your own money, tracking your income and expenses is essential. By understanding exactly where your money goes, you can make better decisions and create a solid foundation for the future.

Whether you prefer using a simple spreadsheet or a budgeting app, building this habit now will make it easier to stay organized as your financial responsibilities grow. Start by tracking all your income and expenses. Knowing how much you're earning and where it's being spent is the first step to managing your finances effectively.

Apps like Mint or Quicken can automate much of the process, but a paper or digital spreadsheet works just as well if you prefer a hands-on approach. In Excel or Google Sheets, create columns for your income, fixed expenses (like rent and utilities), variable expenses (like groceries and entertainment), savings, and debt payments.

Regularly update these categories—whether weekly or monthly—to maintain an accurate picture of your finances. Formulas can help you calculate totals for each category and determine how much money you have left at the end of the month.

If creating a spreadsheet from scratch feels daunting, there are free templates available online that you can customize to fit your needs. By establishing this routine early, you'll not only gain a clear understanding of your financial situation but also build the confidence to make adjustments as needed.

Whether it's cutting back on non-essential spending, setting savings goals, or allocating more to paying off debt, tracking your money gives you the information you need to take control of your financial future.

Monthly Budget

EXPENSE	PLAN	ACTUAL	DIFFERENCE
HOUSING			
Mortgage/Rent			
Maintenance			
UTILITIES			
Electric/gas			
Garbage			
Water			
Cable/satellite			
Internet			
Phone/cell phone			
INSURANCE			
Home			
Automobile			
Health/life			
AUTOMOBILE			
Auto payment			
Fuel			
Maintenance/repairs			
Public transportation			
FOOD			
Groceries			
Meals out			
ENTERTAINMENT			
Movie rentals			
Events			
Travel			
SERVICES			
Medical/dental			
Hair/personal care			
Other: ______			
MISCELLANEOUS			
Clothing			
Toiletries/cosmetics			
Cleaning/laundry			
Pet care			
Other:			
DEBT REPAYMENT			
Loans			
Credit card: ______			
Credit card:			
Other: ______			
CHARITY			
SAVINGS			
Totals:			

		Notes:
Monthly income		
Planned spending		
Actual spending		
Over or under amount		

Understanding the Spreadsheet Above

This template provides a comprehensive monthly budget. It's organized into categories like housing, utilities, and insurance, with columns for planned budget, actual spending, and the difference between the two. By using it, you can manage your expenses, identify overspending, and ensure you're staying on track with your financial goals.

Setting Up Apps Like Quicken

Budgeting apps like Quicken, Mint, or You Need A Budget (YNAB) can simplify managing your finances by automating the process. These tools take the hassle out of tracking expenses and help you stay organized without manually completing and updating spreadsheets.

To get started, download and install an app that fits your needs. Once installed, link your financial accounts, such as your bank accounts and credit cards, to automatically import transactions. This saves you time and ensures accuracy.

Next, categorize your expenses. Most apps will automatically assign transactions to categories like groceries, dining out, or entertainment, but you can customize these if necessary. Once your expenses are organized, set budget goals for each category—for example, $200 for dining out and $500 for groceries.

Make it a habit to review your spending regularly. Checking in weekly or monthly can help you see if you're staying within your goals and make adjustments as needed. These apps are a powerful way to stay on top of your finances with minimal effort, ensuring you're always informed and in control.

The 50/30/20 Rule

The 50/30/20 rule is a straightforward method to manage your income by dividing it into three key categories: needs, wants, and savings. This approach ensures a balanced budget that covers essentials while leaving room for enjoyment and future growth.

Start by allocating 50% of your income to needs. These are the essentials like rent or mortgage payments, groceries, utilities, and other necessary bills. These expenses should take up no more than half of your income to ensure you're living within your means.

Next, dedicate 30% to wants. This category includes non-essential items that bring joy or convenience, such as dining out, streaming subscriptions, and hobbies. It allows you to enjoy life without overspending on luxuries.

The final 20% goes to savings and debt repayment. This portion is vital for building your financial future, including contributions to savings accounts, retirement funds, and paying down loans or credit cards.

By following the 50/30/20 rule, you create a budget that supports your current lifestyle while preparing for the future. It's a simple yet effective way to ensure your financial health remains strong.

Building a Strong Financial Foundation

By implementing strategies like using budgeting apps and following the 50/30/20 rule, you'll set yourself up for success. Starting with manageable steps now, like tracking expenses and allocating income, builds habits that will serve you well throughout your life. Financial security and peace of mind don't happen overnight, but they begin with the intentional choices you make today.

YOUR THIRTIES: BUILDING MOMENTUM

By the time you reach your thirties, your financial life may become more complex. You might be juggling family responsibilities, a mortgage, or other significant commitments. To keep pace, your budget needs to evolve alongside your changing priorities.

Reassess Your Goals

Your priorities may shift as you settle into your career or start a family. Goals like buying a home or saving for your children's education might come into focus, making it essential to revisit and adjust your budget. Start by updating your existing budget or creating a new one using tools like Excel or Google Sheets.

This includes new categories such as childcare, mortgage payments, or college savings. Adjust your income and expense estimates to reflect your current financial situation. Simplify calculations by using built-in functions like "sum" to ensure your income covers all expenses while still allowing room for savings. Revisiting your budget regularly keeps you on track with your evolving priorities.

Increase Retirement Contributions

As your income grows, aim to increase your retirement contributions to at least 15% of your earnings, counting any employer match. This ensures that your savings keep up with your lifestyle and long-term goals.

Budgeting apps like Quicken or Mint can help simplify this process. Use the app's retirement planning feature to estimate how much you need to save and set monthly contribution goals. Regularly monitor your progress to make adjustments as needed.

Plan for Big Expenses

Preparing for significant upcoming costs—such as a down payment on a house, a new car, or a family vacation—is another critical aspect of financial planning in your thirties. Create separate savings buckets for each goal, prioritizing the most immediate needs first.

Think about future expenses, too, such as home renovations, college tuition, or healthcare costs. Factoring these into your budget now can prevent financial stress later. By breaking these larger expenses into manageable savings goals, you'll be better equipped to handle them when the time comes.

Building a Strong Financial Foundation

Financial complexity is inevitable in your thirties, but it's entirely manageable with a thoughtful approach. This stage of life is about reassessing priorities, increasing retirement savings, and preparing for large expenses. By regularly updating your budget and leveraging tools like Excel, Google Sheets, or budgeting apps, you'll maintain momentum and continue building a secure financial future.

Your Forties and Fifties: Hitting Your Stride

In your forties and fifties, you're likely in or approaching your peak earning years. This stage of life offers a prime opportunity to build significant wealth and position yourself for a comfortable retirement. With careful planning and regular adjustments, you can make the most of this period to secure your financial future.

Maximize Retirement Savings

If you're not already maximizing your retirement contributions, now is the time to start. Make sure you're taking full advantage of tax-deferred accounts like 401(k)s and IRAs. If you're 50 or older, don't forget about catch-up contributions, which let you add extra money to your savings each year.

To stay on track, it's important to keep an eye on your retirement accounts. You can easily do this by creating a simple tracker in Excel or Google Sheets for your 401(k), IRAs, and other accounts. Update it regularly to see how your contributions are adding up. If you're feeling tech-savvy, use tools like the "forecast" function to see how your savings could grow over time with continued contributions and the power of compound interest.

Diversify Investments

As retirement draws closer, diversifying your investments becomes increasingly important to reduce risk and protect your nest egg. Make sure your portfolio includes a balanced mix of stocks, bonds, and other investments that align with your retirement timeline and risk tolerance.

Apps like Quicken can simplify investment tracking. Use its features to monitor your portfolio and regularly review your asset allocation. Adjust as needed to ensure your investments remain diversified and appropriate for your financial goals.

Update Your Budget

Your budget will likely evolve during this stage of life as your financial priorities shift. For example, you might have children going off to college, or you may be paying off your mortgage. Redirect any freed-up funds toward retirement savings or other long-term goals to make the most of these changes.

It's also important to revisit your budget regularly—at least once a year or after major life events—to ensure it still aligns with your current financial situation and goals. Don't forget to account for inflation, particularly in areas like groceries, utilities, and healthcare, to maintain your purchasing power as prices rise over time.

Building Wealth and Security

In your forties and fifties, you have a unique opportunity to make significant strides toward a secure and enjoyable retirement. By maximizing your retirement savings, diversifying your investments, and keeping your budget up to date, you can build wealth effectively during these peak earning years. These strategies ensure you're well-prepared to transition into retirement with confidence and the financial stability to support your ideal lifestyle.

Retirement: Enjoying the Fruits of Your Labor

When you finally reach retirement, it's time to enjoy the results of your hard work and careful planning. However, budgeting doesn't stop here. Your focus will shift toward maintaining your lifestyle and ensuring your savings last throughout your retirement years.

Estimate Your Retirement Expenses

Your expenses in retirement will likely differ from when you were working. Begin by estimating what you'll need for essentials like housing, food, and healthcare. Don't forget to include discretionary spending for travel, hobbies, and entertainment. Some costs, like work-related clothing or commuting, may decrease, freeing up funds for the activities you enjoy.

To manage your retirement budget effectively, use whatever system you're comfortable with, whether that's a spreadsheet program, an app, or even a notebook. Create a dedicated space to organize categories for basic living costs, travel, healthcare, and fun activities. Enter estimated costs based on your current spending habits and anticipated changes, and ensure your total expenses align with your retirement income.

Withdraw Strategically

Making your savings last requires a thoughtful withdrawal strategy. Plan your withdrawals to minimize taxes and maximize growth. For example, consider withdrawing from taxable accounts first to allow your tax-deferred accounts, like IRAs and 401(k)s, to continue growing.

Budgeting apps like Quicken can help track your withdrawals and retirement income. Set up withdrawal plans within the app and monitor your progress to ensure your spending stays aligned with your financial goals.

Adjust for Inflation

Inflation can erode your purchasing power over time, so it's crucial to account for rising costs. Investments like Treasury Inflation-Protected Securities (TIPS) can help safeguard your retirement funds against inflation.

Regularly revisit your budget and spending categories, particularly for areas like groceries, utilities, and healthcare, where inflation can have a significant impact. Updating your retirement projections to reflect inflation ensures that your savings remain sufficient to cover your expected living expenses.

Keep Track and Stay Flexible

Your retirement budget isn't static. Life circumstances can shift unexpectedly, such as health challenges or changes in income. Regularly track your spending and be prepared to make adjustments as needed. If you find yourself overspending, identify areas where you can cut back without compromising your quality of life.

Flexibility is key to maintaining financial stability in retirement. Embrace changes as they come and adapt your budget to suit your evolving needs, ensuring you can enjoy a secure and fulfilling retirement.

Living the Life You've Planned

Retirement is about more than just numbers; it's about living the life you've envisioned while staying financially secure. By estimating your expenses, planning your withdrawals wisely, accounting for inflation, and staying flexible, you can enjoy the freedom and joy that retirement offers while ensuring your savings last for the long haul.

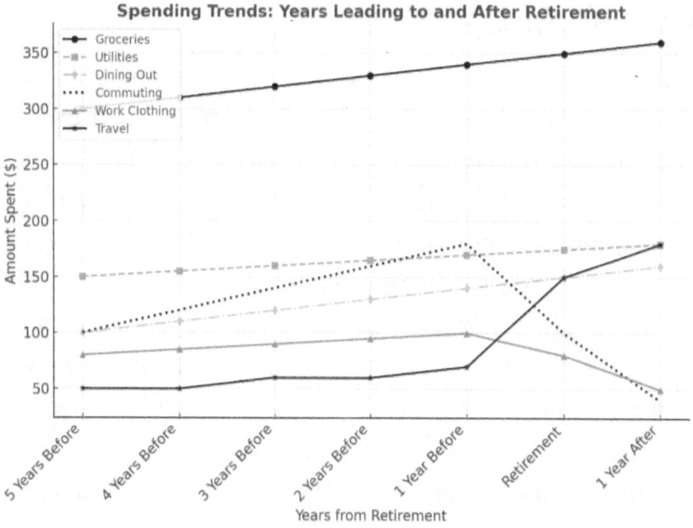

Understanding the Graph Above

This graph highlights spending trends across various categories as you approach and transition into retirement. It demonstrates how certain expenses, like commuting and work attire, tend to peak during your working years but decrease significantly once you retire.

On the other hand, categories such as travel often see a notable increase during retirement as you embrace the freedom to explore and pursue leisure activities. Recognizing these shifts is essential for effective retirement planning. It allows you to anticipate changes in your spending habits and adjust your budget accordingly. By preparing for these transitions, you can manage your finances wisely and ensure a comfortable, enjoyable retirement.

Closing Thoughts

Budgeting isn't a one-time chore—it's an ongoing journey that grows and adapts with you. By starting small in your twenties and fine-tuning your approach as life unfolds, you can build a solid foundation for a secure and rewarding retirement. It's not about perfection; it's about steady, meaningful progress toward your goals.

Regularly tracking your finances and updating your budget gives you the clarity to make confident decisions, adapt to unexpected changes, and ensure your financial future aligns with your dreams. These habits are your roadmap to navigating life's twists and turns while keeping your goals in sight.

Ready to get started? Take that first step today. Whether it's downloading a budgeting app, setting up a system you'll stick with, or simply reviewing your expenses, every action brings you closer to the life you've envisioned. Remember, your future self will look back and thank you for the thoughtful steps you're taking now.

A Quick Takeaway:

Wealth isn't just about how much you make—it's about how wisely you use what you have.

CONCLUSION

YOUR NEXT STEPS TO A FULFILLING RETIREMENT

As I look back on everything we've covered, one thing stands out: retirement planning doesn't have to be boring! Sure, financial planning is important—nobody wants to live off instant noodles in their golden years—but the real magic of retirement is in balancing work, wealth, joy, and purpose. Let's face it: life is too short to stress over spreadsheets without a little fun thrown in.

Over the years, I've learned that building wealth is only half the story. The other half? It's finding what lights you up—whether it's salsa dancing, baking the perfect sourdough, or finally taking that trip to see the world's largest ball of yarn. A good retirement plan isn't just about stepping away from work; it's about stepping into the life you've always imagined.

That's why this book is more than just a guide to retirement planning. It's part of my larger mission to inspire intentional and purposeful living. My blog, *"Dispensing Life-Changing Words,"* reflects my hope that each reader will find ideas that spark hope, courage, and a commitment to personal growth. Retirement isn't just the end of a career; it's the beginning of a new chapter filled with possibilities.

And here's a little secret: planning early isn't just smart—it's freeing. Starting now means you can laugh more later, whether it's at your own jokes or the fact that you still can't remember why you walked into the kitchen. Retirement isn't just about having enough money to keep the lights on. It's about keeping your inner light shining with experiences, relationships, and maybe a goofy hobby or two.

So, as you plan for the future, don't forget to sprinkle in some fun along the way. Find what makes you smile and let that guide your decisions. Dance in your living room, dream big, and save like your future self is counting on you. Retirement is your time to shine—whether you're hiking mountains, rewatching your favorite sitcoms, or mastering the art of karaoke.

Here's to a retirement that's secure, joyful, and full of laughter. May your future be as extraordinary—and as fun—as you've dreamed! And hey, if nothing else, at least you'll have a solid plan to buy all the ice cream you want. Cheers!

ABOUT THE AUTHOR

WHY I WROTE THIS FOR YOU

Nestled along Cleveland's North Coast, Jay Nesbit is an award-winning author, content creator, and behavioral health pharmacist who's passionate about inspiring purposeful living. With a pharmacy degree from The Ohio State University and an MBA from Texas A&M University - Corpus Christi, Jay blends expertise, empathy, and enthusiasm into his transformative work.

Jay's books, *Rise Above the Rut* and *Small Changes Big Results*, reflect his mission to help readers navigate life's challenges and embrace their dreams. At the heart of his approach is his innovative 3-Step Process, designed to turn aspirations into achievable goals, all while keeping things relatable and down-to-earth.

In addition to his writing, Jay has shaped future pharmacists as a Clinical Assistant Professor of Pharmacy Practice, sharing his knowledge and experience with the next generation.

When he's not penning blog posts or dreaming up the next chapter of his upcoming book, Jay enjoys soaking up the melodies of the Cleveland Orchestra at Severance Hall and marveling at the masterpieces in the Cleveland Museum of Art with his partner, Joyce. He also finds inspiration at the Chautauqua Institution in New York, where lifelong learning takes center stage.

Jay's life isn't all work and no play—he's a self-professed bookworm with a love for both fiction and non-fiction, as well as a music enthusiast who jams to smooth jazz and classic rock. His mantra is simple but profound: "Live with intention, express gratitude, uplift others, and stand by my commitments."

Join Jay on his mission to inspire purposeful living. Connect with him on his Facebook Author Page: www.facebook.com/JayNesbitAuthor and explore more of his insights on his website: www.jaynesbit.com.

The Pharmacist Wordsmith

Dispensing Life-Changing Words.

www.jaynesbit.com

For a more in-depth discussion on living a meaningful life, please check out my first book – *Rise Above the Rut*

Find it on Amazon and at all major book retailers

Thank You!

I'd be truly grateful if you could take a moment to leave an honest review of this book, or any of my books, on Amazon.

Your feedback plays a crucial role in helping other readers discover my books. Together, we can share the message of creating a *Life Well Lived.*

Thank you for your support!

Click on this link to leave your review if you purchased a print book on Amazon.com
https://www.amazon.com/gp/your-account/order-history

And follow these steps:

1. Click the link above
2. Sign in to Amazon if prompted
3. Find my book – If you've purchased a lot of items on Amazon after my book, you may need to scroll down a bit. Click on 'Write a Product Review'
4. Select a star rating
5. Write a few short words (or long words, I won't judge) and add a title for your review
6. Click the 'submit' button

If you purchased a Kindle digital version of the book

1. Click on 'Returns & Orders' at the top-right of the Amazon page
2. Click on 'Digital Orders' below 'Your Orders'
3. Same as steps 3-6 above

YOUR SPECIAL GIFT OFFER: WIN A FREE AUTOGRAPHED BOOK!

Thank you for purchasing *The 7 Benefits of Retirement Planning*! As a token of my appreciation, I'm thrilled to offer you an exclusive chance to win a **signed copy** of one of my two award-winning books: *Rise Above the Rut* or *Small Changes Big Results*.

Here's how it works:

- **24 autographed copies are available**.
- Winners are chosen **randomly every month** while supplies last.
- It's completely **FREE to enter**—just register below!
- **PLUS, THERE'S MORE:**

Also, when you sign up, you'll also receive my **"Life-Changing Words"** blog posts straight to your inbox, twice a month. Each post is packed with practical tips, inspiring stories, and actionable advice to help you live a life of purpose and joy.

Take the next step:

Don't miss out on this exciting opportunity! Whether you're looking to create a purposeful life or add an inspiring read to your bookshelf, make sure to register now for your chance to win a free autographed book.

Scan the QR code below to register for your chance to win a free autographed book and receive twice-monthly blog posts filled with inspiration and practical tips. Don't miss this incredible opportunity!

Or visit my website at: https://www.jaynesbit.com/contact

YOUR FREE GIFT

As a way of saying thanks for your purchase, I'm offering the ***Welcome to Your Planning, Living, and Thriving in Retirement Cheat Sheet*** for **FREE** to my readers.

Get instant access!

https://tinyurl.com/FreeResourceDownload

Inside the Free Cheat Sheet, you will discover:

- **Retirement Clarity** – Define your vision and create a plan that fits your goals.
- **Financial Confidence** – Budget, save, and invest wisely for a secure future.
- **Meaningful Living** – Stay active, engaged, and fulfilled in retirement.

If you want practical strategies to plan, live, and thrive in retirement with less stress and more purpose, make sure to grab the free book.

www.ingramcontent.com/pod-product-compliance
Lightning Source LLC
LaVergne TN
LVHW100300210926
848480LV00003B/978
9798230429265